# TABLE OF CONTENTS

# 1. LIVE AID

There was a time when politicians could be excellent orators. This century has seen a significant decline in the arts. One of the few remaining professions in which an individual or group can hold an audience in the palm of their hand, directing a crowd of thousands with their voice, is rock 'n' roll. Film performers are incapable of doing so. Television celebrities don't even come close. Perhaps this is why the rock star is the last great fascinating figure of our time. This occurred to me as I stood in the curtained wings of Wembley Stadium with Who bassist John Entwistle and his fiancée Max on Live Aid day. We witnessed Freddie play in front of about 80,000 people and a television viewership of. ..What are the chances? In the years since, various figures have been floated, ranging from '400 million in around 50 countries via satellite' to '1.9 billion worldwide'. He gave it the works with nonchalance, wit, cheek, and sex. We stood there, mouths open. Any attempt to speak to them was drowned out by the thunderous clamour of the throng. Freddie couldn't care less. The raw power that held his audience riveted was so strong, you could almost smell it. Backstage, the biggest names in music took a break to watch their competitor steal the show. Freddie understood exactly what he was doing. This improbable king and queen dominated the globe for eighteen minutes.

We create luck in a variety of ways. Bob Geldof was lucky to be jotting in his diary in a taxi one day. It was November 1984. Rudimentary lyrics that would soon rock the world emerged from the depths of his brain, a 'battleground of opposing thoughts,' as he later characterised it. It happened shortly after seeing Michael Buerk's harrowing BBC News report from famine-ravaged Ethiopia. Fearful after seeing a television video showing biblical levels of misery, Geldof felt both stunned and helpless, his intuition telling him that he had to get involved. He didn't know how. He could do what he did best: sit down and write a smash tune, with the proceeds going to Oxfam. However, his Irish punk band The Boomtown Rats were in decline at the time, having not had a Top Ten single since 1980. Their peak, a number one with 'I Don't Like Mondays,' had passed them by in 1979. He recognized that if the musician was big enough, music fans would flock to buy a charity song, especially around the

4

# Freddie Mercury

## Biography

### Shining star in the rock music scene

**Scott Dolejs**

Christmas season. It was just a matter of finding a sympathetic star to record one with. How much better would it be if he could get the entire galaxy to sing along to one song?

Bob chatted with Midge Ure, whose band Ultravox were performing that week on The Tube, a Channel 4 rock and pop show hosted by Geldof's then-girlfriend (and soon-to-be wife), the late Paula Yates. Midge agreed to compose several arrangements and set Geldof's lyrics to music. Bob then visited Sting, Simon Le Bon of Duran Duran, Gary and Martin Kemp of Spandau Ballet. His galaxy-spanning list grew to include, among others, Boy George, Frankie Goes To Hollywood, The Style Council's Paul Weller, George Michael, and Andrew Ridgeley of Wham! as well as Paul Young. Status Quo's Francis Rossi and Rick Parfitt went in freely. Phil Collins and Bananarama quickly followed. David Bowie and Paul McCartney, who were both present, contributed remotely. These were sent to Geldof to be later dubbed onto the track. Sir Peter Blake, best known for his work on The Beatles' Sgt Pepper's Lonely Hearts Club Band album cover, was commissioned to design the record jacket. Band Aid was created, the name of a play on a popular brand of sticking plaster. This was supposed to be a 'band' that would 'help' the globe.

'Do They Realise It's Christmas?' was recorded at Trevor Horn's Sarm West Studios in Notting Hill, West London, for free on November 25, 1984, and published four days later.

That week's number one was a knockout Scottish vocalist, Jim Diamond, with his magnificent, ageless ballad 'I Should Have Known Better'. Jim's band PhD had a hit with 'I Won't Let You Down' in 1982, but he had never had a solo single. When big-hearted Jim gave an interview about his chart triumph, the music business was stunned.

'I'm pleased to be Number One,' he added, 'but next week I don't want people to buy my record. Instead, I want them to donate to Band Aid.'

'I couldn't believe it,' Geldof remarked. 'As a singer who hadn't had a number one in five years, I knew what that cost him. He'd just tossed away his first hit for the sake of others. It was truly unselfish.'

'Do They Know It's Christmas?' appeared the following week.' sailed straight to Number One in the United Kingdom, outselling everything else on the chart and became the country's fastest-selling song since the list's establishment in 1952. In the first week alone, a million copies were sold. The song was number one for five weeks and sold over three and a half million copies. It went on to become the UK's best-selling single of all time, ending Queen's nine-year dominance with the 'ba-rock' 'Bohemian Rhapsody'. 'Do They Realise It's Christmas?'Candle in the Wind/Something About the Way You Look Tonight', re-recorded as a memorial to the late Princess of Wales, would only be outsold in 1997 by Elton John's double-A-side charity single.

'Queen were really disappointed that they had not been invited to appear on "Do They Know It's Christmas?"Spike Edney, a session musician who toured with Queen as the band's fifth member, contributing on keyboards, vocals, and rhythm guitar, and who had earned his career performing for The Boomtown Rats and a slew of other big-known acts, acknowledges as much.

'I was on a Rats tour with Bob and stated this to him. He then told me that he was hoping to put on a spectacle and that he would surely ask Queen to perform. "Bollocks," I remember thinking. He's insane. It will never happen."'

The industry's reaction to Geldof's achievements thus far suggested otherwise. Following closely behind the British chart attempt was America's contribution, in the form of supergroup USA for Africa and their hit "We Are the World." The session, which was written by Michael Jackson and Lionel Richie and produced by Quincy Jones and Michael Omartian, brought together some of the world's most iconic musicians. It was recorded in January 1985 in Hollywood's A & M Studios and featured a remarkable ensemble that included Diana Ross, Bruce Springsteen, Smokey Robinson, Cyndi Lauper, Billy Joel, Dionne Warwick, Willey Nelson, and Huey Lewis. More than forty-five of America's best musicians participated in total. Another fifty people had to be turned away. When the chosen ones came to the studio, they were greeted by a notice that said, "Please check your egos at the door." They were also greeted by an arrogant Stevie Wonder, who informed them that if the song wasn't up to scratch or down in one take, he and fellow blind musician Ray Charles would drive them all home. The tune sold over 20 million copies and became America's fastest-selling pop hit of all time.

Following Queen's challenging The Works performance, Geldof stepped up his charity drive, stating ambitions to build the most ambitious rock 'n' roll endeavour of all time. Queen did not consider themselves an obvious choice for the concert lineup because they had been ignored for the single. That now appears to be an irony. Despite a fifteen-year career, an unrivalled back catalogue of albums, singles, and videos, royalties in the millions, and having won the majority of music awards thanks to musicianship that embraced rock, pop, opera, rockabilly, disco, funk, and folk, Queen's star appeared to be fading. The band had been gone from home for a long time, between August 1984 and May 1985, promoting their album, The Works, and performed live for 325,000 fans at the Rock in Rio festival in January 1985. However, the trip had been plagued by issues. There had been talk of their splitting up.

'They were plainly drifting,' Spike Edney confirms. 'Times had changed, and we had entered a completely new musical genre. Everything was New Romantics, Spandau Ballet, and Duran Duran. There are no guarantees or accounts for success or failure. For a while, things had been going wrong for the Queen, particularly in America. There was some nonsense going on with their US label. Their self-esteem was shaken. Maybe they took it out on each other a little. Who wouldn't want to?'

'Hey, people quarrel,' says Rick Wakeman, their close friend and former Strawb and Yes-man.

'Band members disagree. It's understandable: how many other professions do you have where you're constantly thrown together? You eat breakfast together, commute to work together, and eat every meal together while on the road. The only time you're alone is in bed, and even then it's not always. No matter how pleasant you are, there will come a point when you will think to yourself, "If that guy scratches his head one more time, I'll stick a knife in him." You must learn to give each other room. It doesn't matter if one gets pissed, goes to a drug den, makes it to the arena to practise, or nips off to a football match if you compose the appropriate music. When you gather a group of four or five extreme creatives who do beautiful things with their thoughts, hands, and voices together, there's a lot of potential for pyrotechnics. The Queen was no different than the rest of us in that regard.'

After touring to promote their perplexingly dance-y, guitar-less 1982 album Hot Space, Freddie Mercury, Brian May, Roger Taylor, and John Deacon effectively separated to pursue individual projects, most notably Brian with Eddie Van Halen on the Star Fleet Project and Freddie on his own. They reformed in Los Angeles in August 1983 to work on The Works, their ninth studio album and debut CD. The first single was "Radio Ga Ga." The Works also included the hard-rock tune 'Hammer to Fall' and the melancholy ballad 'Is This the World We Created. ..?', as well as the contentious 'I Want to Break Free,' with its outlandish cross-dressing video based on a domestic scene from the British TV drama Coronation Street. While the single was enormously successful in the United Kingdom and other regions, it offended conservative Middle America and upset many fans.

Worse, Queen, along with Rod Stewart, Rick Wakeman, Status Quo, and others, had recently violated the United Nations cultural boycott by performing in apartheid South Africa. The band received substantial criticism for their October 1984 performances at Sun City, Sol Kerzner's casino, golf, and entertainment complex in Botswana, and were fined and blacklisted by the British Musicians' Union. This was a tragedy for an African-born performer like Freddie. The matter was not resolved until 1993, a year before Nelson Mandela was elected President of South Africa. In later years, Queen would become a big and ardent supporter of Mandela.

'I completely supported the Queen when they went to South Africa,' Rick Wakeman responds. 'I, too, gave a concert in the midst of apartheid with an ensemble of black Zulus, Asians, and whites.

'I did a Journey to the Center of the Earth down there, and I was crucified by the British press. I tried to explain, but they weren't interested. It's not "black" or "white" music; it's just an orchestra or a choir. Playing there did not imply support for the apartheid administration. George Benson visited there. Diana Ross visited there. How come people of colour could perform but whites couldn't? That is racist in and of itself. "For fuck's sake, I'm half-black and half-Welsh, how bad can it be?" said Shirley Bassey." So when the Queen went to South Africa, I was overjoyed. They brought attention to the foolishness of it all, as well as the truth that music has no sexual, cultural, or ethnic limitations. It applies to everyone.'

On July 13, 1985, Live Aid's 'global jukebox' would be staged in two massive arenas. Wembley Stadium in London and John F. Kennedy Stadium in Philadelphia have both been reserved. The organisation proved to be a logistical nightmare.

'I assumed Bob was joking when he first came into my office to discuss this event,' recalls promoter Harvey Goldsmith. 'There were no fax machines, computers, cell phones, or anything else in 1985. We were communicating via telex and landlines. I recall sitting in my office one afternoon with a large satellite map and a pair of antique callipers, attempting to predict where the satellite would be at various times. When we went to the BBC, Bob thumped the table and said, "I want seventeen hours of television" - it was revolutionary. We might use the BBC's commitment as leverage to encourage broadcasters all across the world to do the same. It was the first time something like this had ever happened. It was my duty to put the parts together and make it work.'

Then there was the task of convincing rock's biggest names, some of whom had already contributed to the recording of the charity singles, to perform and help raise even more money for the dying. This was to be a spectacularly brazen reprisal by the music industry against governments all across the world that had failed to act.

'This was the dickheads in rock 'n' roll, just getting on with it,' says Francis Rossi of Status Quo. When I look back, it makes me angry. I believe that if everyone had worked together - if we had seen the magnitude of what could have been accomplished - we could have persuaded the oil giants, the BPs and Shells and others, to do their part. We could have made a hundred times what we raised. Don't tell me the government couldn't have passed legislation to address concerns like advertising and so on. All major corporations might have gotten engaged, and the outcome would have been massive. It was an uncharted area at the time. Today, we have a fresh perspective on Live Aid. Still, all credit goes to Bob. He put together something that only a few people could have done.'

How did Geldof persuade the Queen to participate?

'Bob encouraged me to ask the band if they'd be interested, which I had the opportunity to do while Queen was on tour in New Zealand,' Spike Edney adds. 'Why doesn't he ask us himself?' they said.'I explained that he was worried they would reject him. They didn't sound convinced, but they stated they'd think about it. I informed Bob, and he officially approached [Queen manager] Jim Beach.'

Geldof then described how he won them over.

'I tracked Jim right down to. .."Look, for Christ's sake, you know, what's wrong with them?" I remarked, referring to some small coastal resort where he was staying." Jim said, "Oh, you know, Freddie's very sensitive," so I said, "Tell the old faggot it's going be the biggest thing that ever occurred - this massive mega thing," and they ultimately got back and said OK, they'd certainly be doing it, and I thought, Great. And when it came to Live Aid, Queen was without a doubt the best band on the planet. Your personal preferences were unimportant. When the big day arrived, they played their best, had the best sound, and made the most of their time. They completely grasped the concept, which I'd presented as a worldwide jukebox. They simply pounded out one hit after another. It was simply incredible. I was actually upstairs in Wembley Stadium's Appeals box when I heard this sound. I thought to myself, "God, who's got this sound together?"'

Geldof had no idea, nor did anybody else at the moment, that immediately before their 6.40 p.m. Queen's sound engineer, James 'Trip' Khalaf, went out front to 'check the system' and fiddled with the limiters covertly.

'We were louder than anyone else at Live Aid,' Roger Taylor admitted. 'You have to overwhelm a stadium crowd!"

'I went outside and noticed it was the Queen,' Geldof explained. I glanced down at this tremendous crowd of people, and the band was incredible. I believe they were overjoyed afterwards, especially Freddie. The entire planet was the ideal platform for him. And he could dance around on stage doing "We Are the Champions" and stuff like that. How much more perfect could it get?'

'We didn't know Bob at all,' John Deacon admitted in a rare interview. "Do They Know It's Christmas?"" was released, which included many of the newer performers. He intended to bring in a lot of established acts for the gig. We couldn't believe it - twenty minutes with no sound check! We'd just finished visiting Japan when it became clear that it was going to happen, and we ended up having supper in the hotel, debating whether we should do it. ..and we agreed. One day, I felt proud to be a part of the music industry. You surely don't feel that way most of the time! But the day was so enjoyable that everyone forgot about the competitiveness. ..It was also a nice morale lift for us because it demonstrated the strength of our support in England as well as what we had to offer as a band.'

'There was nothing particularly remarkable about the way we put the set together,' Spike Edney confesses.

'We all sat around discussing which songs to play and eventually decided on a mix of hits. There's no huge mystery to it - if you have a bunch of tunes and can't decide, it's the natural thing to do. Everything seemed pretty matter-of-fact, despite the excellent time. That band's members are all nightmarish perfectionists. ..That is also a nice thing. It turned out to be great that day.'

'Queen had rehearsed incredibly hard at the Shaw Theatre on [London's] Euston Road for a whole week, while others just went on and busked it,' recalls Freddie's personal assistant, Peter 'Phoebe' Freestone.

'That's why they were the best on that particular day. I recall Freddie being taken aback as he launched into "Radio Ga Ga" and watched thousands of hands go up. He was taken aback by it, having never seen anything like it before. They'd only ever sung that song in the dark.'

Spike Edney, on the other hand, remembers things differently, believing that Freddie was in 'full-blown bring-it-on mode,' and that he and the band took everything in stride. I have to agree with him based on what I witnessed. This was Queen's crowning achievement, the culmination of their entire career.

'Behind the scenes, it was all organised pandemonium,' Spike recounted. 'Backstage, everyone was quite engaging and open. Nobody was being snobbish or attempting to outdo one another. It was like a wonderful summer picnic until the Queen came on. That's not to imply the Queen wasn't calculating and shrewd. They simply carried on as usual, expecting everyone else to do the same. I was taken aback when I heard certain musicians belt out their latest single: that's not your target audience! That was not done by the Queen. They simply carried out Bob's request. The "greatest rock performance of all time," as it is now commonly referred to. What exactly does that mean? What it was, in fact, was a band at the top of their game performing what they did best and shocking everyone.'

'No one was prepared. ..except Queen,' says Pete Smith, the show's global event coordinator and author of Live Aid. 'I watched the set on the backstage monitors. The BBC had placed TV monitors throughout the artist area. These TVs, along with the several clocks that Harvey had bought, kept everyone informed of where we were in the proceedings. Queen ripped up the rule book and rewrote it in twenty minutes. The impact was tangible. Live Aid was now on the gas.'

Queen's reputation on the world stage was on the wane even when they were at their spectacular best both musically and technically - there was no more professional rock band in existence at the time. Their popularity had dipped as a result of a slew of miscalculations, blunders, and a general, broad shift in musical tastes. The Queen was starting to think they'd had their day. A permanent division was planned. They'd discussed it. All of this was about to change thanks to Live Aid.

But what made their amazing performance so memorable? Spike Edney, for one, couldn't get it.

'This was what the Queen stood for!' He chuckled. 'They were well known all over the world for putting on a fantastic show and giving it their all. They weren't exactly rookies when it came to stadium gigs. This was their natural environment, and the larger the crowd, the better. They could probably do this in their sleep. To be honest, the Queen was surprised that everyone else was surprised! It was just another day at the office for them. Having said that, we knew we'd done it when we got off the plane. The Queen discovered that their entire world had changed after Live Aid.'

Bernard Doherty oversaw the event's publicity, handling all media on the day.

'We knew we had to keep the press happy in order to get maximum coverage. I only had eight triple-A laminate passes, but hundreds of pieces of press. We had to distribute them. One by one I said to everyone: "Right, you've got forty-five minutes in there, get what you can, get back out. See you in the Hard Rock Café", of which there was a "branch" backstage. Backstage was a wagon-train-style scenario, with all the artists' Portacabins pointing inwards, and Elton cooking a barbecue somewhere in the thick of it all because he didn't fancy the offerings of the café. David Bailey set his photo studio up in a stinky little corner, he wasn't proud. Nobody's conditions were ideal. It was all thrown together on the fly. But somehow it happened. Everyone got in the spirit of the thing, most people left their egos at home, and it worked.'

At the time, Doherty had David Bowie as a client, and was obliged to take care of his needs too.

'Always a little nerve-wracking when you are looking after your artist and doing two jobs at once. In my case, that day, about eighteen jobs. There wasn't much love lost between David and Elton – they'd obviously fallen out. David came out of his performance OK. Elton did all right. The one musician David was genuinely pleased to see was Freddie. They really were delighted to be together again. They stood chatting, as if they'd only seen each other yesterday. The affection between them was tangible. David was wearing an amazing blue suit, and looked incredibly sharp and healthy. Just before David went on, Freddie winked at him and said, "If I didn't know you better, dear, I'd have to eat you." No wonder David went out on stage with such a big smile on his face.'

All day long, Freddie remained relaxed.

'He sat holding court, in that perfectly camp but quite humble way of his,' agrees Bernard. 'He knew the power he had over people, but it didn't go to his head. If he'd been sitting outside a beach hut in Southend-on-Sea, he'd have taken people's breath away. He was a true star, with that indefinable quality. John Deacon I wasn't aware of, where was he? And I didn't see Brian May or Roger Taylor speak to each other all day. They were like a divorced couple at the same party.'

Quo's Francis Rossi disagrees.

'I don't subscribe to the theory that the Queen was on the point of breaking up then. They seemed like they were getting on all right to me, and we knew the boys in the band pretty well. All bands have differences. They were certainly united in their commitment to the Live Aid cause.'

The backstage area was nonetheless rife with rumours about Queen being on the verge of breaking up.

'It showed,' insists Bernard Doherty.

'Not when they went on, though. If there were differences, they were intelligent enough to put them aside to get on with the job in hand. And they went out there and won. Queen had the wow factor. What else do we remember about Live Aid? The sound going down on The Who. Bono getting in the zone, losing the plot and confounding the others by breaking the rules of performance that day – none of the rest of U2 would talk to him after that.'

Despite Live Aid turning out to be the performance that established U2 as a stadium group with a superstar future, it almost went horribly wrong. Not only did they play a self-indulgent fourteen-minute version of their 'heroin song' 'Bad', from the 1984 album The Unforgettable Fire, but Bono punctuated it riskily with blasts of Lou Reed's 'Satellite of Love' and 'Walk on the Wild Side', as well as by bits from The Rolling Stones' 'Ruby Tuesday' and 'Sympathy for the Devil'. This left room for only one other song, causing their finale 'Pride (In the Name of Love)', an eventual global mega-hit, to be ditched. Then Bono spotted a young girl being crushed in the crowd when the audience, reacting to the singer's charisma, surged forwards. Although he signalled desperately to stadium stewards to save her, they failed to understand. So Bono took a leap of faith thirty feet down into the throng to pick her up himself – and wound up dancing with her. What emerged from the experience was how brilliantly Bono connected with an audience. That brief dance, sealed with a kiss, became an indelible image of Live Aid, resulting in all of U2's albums re-entering the UK charts.

'On the day, though, they really thought they'd blown it,' said Doherty. 'Simon Le Bon did blow it, with the bum note of all time. Then there were the critics drooling over Bowie. Phil Collins, playing both Wembley and JFK courtesy of Concorde – though I think a lot of people wished he hadn't bothered, not least the hastily re-formed Led Zeppelin, who he drummed for at JFK. As for the Queen, they did exactly what Bob had asked them to do. I watched from the wings and I was blown away. I was behind Freddie, looking over his shoulder onto the piano, just a couple of feet away from him. I stood watching the audience with some trepidation. You never know: even the greatest acts in the world bomb, and you don't know why.'

We needn't have worried. The Queen drew from every influence, every which way. They gave it all they had. So many other supreme performers flooded back into my mind at that point: Alex Harvey, the great glam rocker of the Sensational Alex Harvey Band. Ian Dury and the Blockheads. Mick Jagger. Ziggy Stardust and the Spiders. What Freddie displayed better than on perhaps any other occasion was instinctive star quality, as well as a phenomenal grasp of what makes a must-watch show. He conjured up all the genius of Vaudeville. It was as if he had studied and absorbed the best-kept secrets of every definitive artist who had gone before him, and sorcerer a little of all those greats into his own act. It was quite a formula. The ultimate peacock, Freddie seduced us all.

Not, admits Doherty, that he knew Queen were making history that day.

'Not on the day, no. I had headphones on, and a walkie-talkie – no mobile phones back then. I was worrying about Dave Hogan and Richard Young in the pit. I had Bob and Harvey to fret about. It was all going on, I had a lot on my mind. I knew the band was going down well, sure. The crowd was going nuts. Everyone backstage stopped talking to watch them. That was bizarre. Never normally happens . ..Who came on before or after Queen? Hardly anyone remembers. What do I remember? Freddie Mercury was the greatest performer on the day. Perhaps the greatest performer ever.'

David Wigg, the veteran journalist then writing for the Daily Express, had long been a close personal friend of Freddie's.

'I was the only journalist allowed to join Freddie in his dressing room as he prepared for Queen's performance at the biggest show in the world,' he says. 'He was very relaxed, and looking forward to getting out there to do his bit.'

'We are playing songs that people identify with, to make it a happy occasion,' Freddie had explained.

Freddie and David discussed the reasons behind Live Aid, and talked about Freddie's own experiences in childhood.

'He said that he first became aware that he was luckier than a lot of children when he attended an English boarding school in India, and discovered through a boy's eyes the plight of the country's poor.'

'But,' Freddie had insisted, 'I'm certainly not doing this out of guilt. I don't feel guilty just because I'm rich. Even if I didn't do it, the problem would still be there. It's something that will sadly always be there. The idea of all this is to make the whole world aware of the fact that this is going on. By making this concert we are doing something positive to make people look, listen, and hopefully donate. Neither should we be looking at it in terms of us and them. When people are starving, it should be looked upon as one united problem.'

Freddie openly admitted to 'Wiggie' that when he saw a TV film of Africa's starving millions, he had to switch off his set.

'It disturbs me so much, I just can't watch it. Sometimes I do feel helpless, and this is one of those times I can do my bit. Bob has done a wonderful thing, because he actually sparked it off. I'm sure we all had it in us to do that, but it took someone like him to become the driving force, and actually get us all to come together.'

For one concert-goer, that day was the most overwhelming for the fact that this was his first rock experience. Jim Hutton, the humble hairdresser who became Freddie's partner shortly before Live Aid, went on to share the rest of Freddie's life. Little could he have known that day that, just six years later, he would be helping to prepare his lover for burial. Conveyed to the concert in grandeur as Freddie's other half in the star's own limousine, it was the first time Jim had ever attended a gig of any kind, let alone watched Queen play live.

'Talk about chucking me in at the deep end,' laughed Jim. 'I was a bit blown away by all the glamorous superstars to be honest. Every member of the band had his own trailer. All the wives were there, as well as Roger's and Brian's children. Freddie knew everyone. He took me to meet David Bowie, who I'd actually met before, when I cut his hair. He even introduced me to Elton John as "my new man". Freddie didn't need time to get ready, he was just going on stage in what he was wearing when we left home – a white vest with a pair of faded jeans. He also had on a pair of his favourite trainers, a belt and a studded amulet. When it was their turn to go on, he knocked back another large vodka tonic and said, "Let's do it."

'I walked with him to the stage, and kissed him good luck. Not that he needed it. To hear them playing those songs live – a bit of "Bohemian Rhapsody" with Freddie on the piano, "Radio Ga Ga" with the crowd clapping wildly in unison, "Hammer to Fall", then Freddie on his guitar for "Crazy Little Thing Called Love", and "We Will Rock You", and "We Are the Champions", thundering away . ..to a simple guy like me, this was all just mind-boggling. Then later on, once it had got dark, Freddie and Brian back on stage together, just the two of them, performing that wonderful ballad "Is This the World We Created . ..?". They had recorded it quite a while before Live Aid, hadn't they, but it was as if they had written it especially for the occasion. The words were so right, and the way Freddie sang them was just magical. It moved me to tears, as Freddie often did.'

At last, Jim, who died from cancer in January 2010, nineteen years after Freddie's death, had seen his rock-star lover at work.

'He gave it everything up there. He amazed me. Then, when he was off, he seemed glad it was done. "Thank God that's over," he laughed. Another large vodka, and he was calm. We did stay until the end to catch up with everyone, but Freddie didn't want to bother with the after-show party at Legends nightclub. Instead, we went home to Garden Lodge like an old married couple, to watch the rest of the American leg on television.'

Conspicuous by their absence that day were Freddie's own parents. Although often in attendance at Queen's UK concerts, they chose instead to witness this spectacle at home.

'It was such a huge event, it would have been too complicated,' recalled Freddie's mum Jer, suggesting that she and Freddie's father Bomi would have been overwhelmed by both the crowds and the logistics of getting to and from the stadium. So I watched it on television. I was so proud. My husband turned to me and said, "Our boy's done it."'

From the viewpoint of professionals charged with transmitting and recording the event, Freddie's contribution had been little short of sensational. Mike Appleton, former executive producer of The Old Grey Whistle Test – the influential BBC television rock series – remembers Mercury's performance as 'fascinating'.

'For a start, he was not even supposed to go on. Doctors had already said that he was too ill to perform. His throat was terrible, from a cold or something. He wasn't well enough, but he absolutely insisted. It happened that he and Bono of U2 wound up as the most successful performers of the day.

'It was so interesting to see Freddie through the monitors – I was shut away in a sweltering OB truck all day long. We were literally building a programme live on air as we went. Come five o'clock and we were flipping live to JFK – alternating twenty minutes here, twenty minutes there, let's put an interview in here, a live bit from earlier there, some highlights of the first hour in this slot . ..it's actually very exciting television, and the only way I like to work. Freddie simply came on, took immediate possession of the stage, coolly and calmly, and then proceeded to take possession of the audience.

'Queen had at that point been off the boil for a while, having made no significant impact with an album for some time. The Live Aid experience wound up putting them back on the map, and had the same effect on the music business as a whole. Overall, sales went up. Live Aid proved to be a tonic for the entire industry. As Freddie was the out-and-out star of the day, he was undoubtedly the main ingredient of that tonic. He was more dominant that day than I'd ever seen him before. The day may have belonged to Bob emotionally. It definitely belonged to Freddie musically.'

Mike later received the BAFTA Award for Live Aid as Producer of the Best Outside Broadcast.

Dave Hogan, who captured the show in stills, shares Appleton's opinion.

'Only six of us were chosen as Live Aid's official photographers', reveals the fabled Sun lensman known as 'Hogie' (who is no stranger to a splash headline himself – 'Maimed By Madonna' was his Warholian moment).

'We were shooting for the Live Aid souvenir book, so we weren't stopped from going anywhere,' he recalls.

'It was obvious to everyone on the day that Freddie was the main man – but not until he actually got on stage. Freddie wasn't a limelight-grabber when he wasn't on. His behaviour was gentlemanly and low-key, compared to most. No one realised how powerful he was until he went out there. At that point, we knew, this is it. I remember him launching into "Radio Ga Ga". It wasn't even dark, he was whipping up all this magic in daylight. That ocean of fans clapping and stamping together just sent shivers down your spine. For us, it was heaven. This is the moment you want. He stole it. The day was full of fantastic moments – Bono leaping into the crowd, McCartney's first live performance since John Lennon was assassinated. But what I saw Freddie do that day took my breath away. He engaged with every single person present. Total unison. Nobody has done that, before or since. I think he was the only one who could do it.'

Thus, the cream of rock sang and danced to feed the world. It has been repeated ad nauseam that Queen's performance was the most thrilling, the most moving, the most memorable, the most enduring – surpassing as it did the efforts of their greatest rivals.

'By far the most extraordinary,' agrees radio presenter Paul Gambaccini. 'You could sense a frisson backstage as heads rose towards the monitors like dogs hearing a whistle. They were stealing the show, and they would regain a stature they would never lose again.'

The other members of Queen were the first to praise their front man.

'The rest of us played OK, but Freddie was out there and took it to another level,' said Brian, with typical modesty. 'It wasn't just Queen fans. He connected with everyone.'

As he later elaborated to me in an emotional interview at Queen's Pembridge Road offices, 'Live Aid was Freddie. He was unique. You could almost see our music flowing through him. You couldn't ignore him. He was original. Special. It wasn't just our fans we were playing to, it was everyone's fans. Freddie really gave his all.'

Of all Queen's 704 live performances fronted by Freddie, it remains their most iconic, their finest hour. Live Aid gave the band the perfect opportunity to demonstrate that, stripped of props and trappings, of their own lighting rig and sound equipment, of fog and smoke and other special effects, without even the natural magic of dusk and with fewer than twenty minutes in which to prove themselves, they were unchallenged sovereigns who still had what it took to rock the world. They would now embrace the unequivocal fact that Queens were greater than the sum of their parts. They had no way of knowing that their finest hour was already behind them. United in exultation, recommitted to the cause, all thoughts of solo careers shelved – for the moment, at least – they were soon to discover that their glittering, second-chance future with Freddie would be tragically short-lived.

# 2. ZANZIBAR

Perhaps Freddie thought that music audiences in the 1970s were unprepared for a rock artist with African and Indian ancestors. It wouldn't make a difference now. On the contrary, many people would perceive it as a benefit. Today, the more muddled and obscure an artist's cultural and musical history is, the more coveted it is. Things were different back then. It's easy to envision him seeing the facts of his life as out of sync with the image he desired to project. A rock star, by definition, came from California (The Beach Boys), New York (Lou Reed), Florida (Jim Morrison), Mississippi (Elvis Presley), or Washington State (Jimi Hendrix). Liverpool, thanks to The Beatles, was likewise cool, as was London, thanks to Mick Jagger and Keith Richards of The Rolling Stones. White Anglo-Saxons were the favourites, with Black Americans coming in second. It was typical for musicians to conceal the details of their past back then because it facilitated glamour and mystery: the kind of thing that publicity specialists were paid a small sum to create. I realised I'd have to go looking for myself because there was so much conflicting information concerning Freddie's birth and youth.

I flew to Dar es Salaam via Nairobi before boarding a boat to Zanzibar Town across a port teeming with dhows and small fishing canoes. Everything about the setting was foreign. To someone like myself, who was born in the most mundane of backwaters, Freddie's disdain of Zanzibar seemed perplexing. The prospect of him regaling his dinner companions with tales of Ali Baba and Sinbad, of wild Arabian princes and Eastern promise galore, is alluring. Why didn't he do it? There had to be a purpose for this. Having an 'enchanted past' was so Freddie.

Zanzibar, a speck in the atlas, is located just south of the Equator off Africa's east coast. Closer inspection reveals two specks: the main island, Unguja, and the more secluded Pemba, a favourite European honeymoon destination today. They currently comprise the United Republic of Tanzania, along with Tanganyika, a neighbouring former German and later British territory. Zanzibar has undergone far more corruption, disruption, and massacre than is possibly fair for such a small region. Over the centuries, it has been invaded by Assyrians, Sumerians, Egyptians, Phoenicians, Indians, Persians, and Arabs, as well as Malays, Chinese, Portuguese, Dutch, and British. Some stayed to settle and dominate, most notably the Shirazi Persians from what is now Southern Iran, the Omani Arabs, and, much later, the British. The Swahili civilization here dates back to the first Islamic awakenings. Zanzibar's spice industry began with the introduction of the clove tree in 1818. Ginger, nutmeg, vanilla, cloves, and cardamom were among the first spices to be exported over the world. Tales of harems, palace intrigues, and royal elopements added to its romanticism as missionaries and adventurers passed through its portals en route to the Dark Continent. It gained a terrible reputation as a thriving ivory and human trafficking trade centre. Until abolition in 1897, 50,000 Africans each year were hauled through its savage market, drawn from as far away as the continent's central lakes, to be flogged as slaves in both senses.

On Unguja's coastlines, there are majestic sultan's palaces, an antique Arab fort with rusty cannons, colonial buildings, and merchants' houses, some under refurbishment, some beyond repair. Behind these are mazes of bazaars and small lanes crowded with houses. For the first eighteen years of Freddie's life, he lived in a Stone Town flat with a view of the sea.

His mother, Jer, was only a child herself when she gave birth to him in Zanzibar's Government Hospital on Thursday, September 5, 1946 - Parsee New Year's Day. It was a godsend that the small eighteen-year-old's first child was a boy. Bomi was overjoyed when the news reached her husband at work. The family name would live on. At least, they assumed it would, blissfully unaware of the lifestyle choices that lay ahead. The couple discussed possible names for their child. Their options as Parsees - practitioners of the monotheistic Zoroastrian faith dating back to early sixth century BC Persia - were restricted. They settled in Farrokh, which Bomi duly registered at the Government Records Office according to legal decree.

'I remember when Freddie was born very clearly,' Perviz Darunkhanawala, née Bulsara, informed me when I paid her a visit at her house in Shangani district. Perviz was the niece of Bomi Bulsara. Sorabji's father and Freddie's father were two of eight brothers.

'Freddie's father and I were both born and raised in Bulsar, a little village north of Bombay [now Mumbai] in the Indian state of Gujarat,' she revealed.

'That's how they came up with the name Bulsara. The brothers arrived in Zanzibar one after the other, looking for a job. My father was hired by Cable and Wireless. Bomi accepted a position as a cashier for the British Government in the High Court. Bomi was not yet married when he arrived in Zanzibar. He returned to India later and married Freddie's mother Jer in Bombay. He then brought her here, where Freddie was born.

'He was so little, almost like a pet. He used to visit my house with his parents even when he was a very tiny infant. They used to go out and leave him with my mother. He used to play around in our house when he was a little older. He was such a mischievous child. I was considerably older than him, and I enjoyed looking after him. He was a young boy, but a very nice child. I was madly in love with him. I wished he would remain every time he came. But his parents would always come and get him at the conclusion of an evening out.'

Perviz observed how the Bulsaras had a very sophisticated social life despite their strict religion and customs. Bomi was able to finance a comfortable home and domestic servants, including Freddie's ayah (nanny), Sabine, on an income that would have characterised him as little more than a humble civil servant in Britain. The family had all they needed, and the weather was pleasant. Kashmira was born in 1952, when Freddie was six years old.

Bomi Bulsara worked out of the non-residential Beit-el Ajaib, or House of Wonders, which Sultan Sayyid Barghash erected in the late nineteenth century for ceremonial purposes. It was once the tallest edifice in East Africa, with magnificent floral gardens. Following a brief insurrection, it was bombarded by a British navy and eventually underwent substantial renovations to become Zanzibar's primary museum. Bomi's employment required him to travel throughout the colony and into India, which may have impacted his decision to send his lone kid to school so far away. However, there was also the issue of how far the child's education could be taken at home. Farrokh attended the Zanzibar Missionary School from the age of five, where his teachers were Anglican nuns, although his parents continued to practise Zoroastrianism. He was considered brighter than normal and showed early talent for painting, drawing, and modelling.

'He was soon maturing into a delightfully respectful, serious, and exact young child,' Perviz recalls.

'He had a glint in his eye and a mischievous streak that would get the better of him every now and then. But I recall him as being secretive and introverted. Embarrassingly shy. Even when he came to meet us with his parents, he didn't say anything. That was his personality. We didn't see each other as much as we used to because he was out playing on the streets and at the beach with all the other lads.'

'He was a really happy young boy who liked music,' his mother Jer remembered. 'Folk, opera, and classical music were all favourites of his. I believe he has always wanted to be a showman.'

Perviz was astonished to find that my attempts to obtain a copy of her cousin's birth certificate from official sources had failed. Even a meeting with the chief registrar yielded no positive results.

'Are you here to obtain Freddie Mercury's birth certificate?'He grinned. 'It isn't here. It had arrived. A woman from Argentina arrived a few years ago to look for it. A copy was created for her, and the original has not been seen since, despite being requested on multiple occasions - I assume by his fans. The fundamental issue is that accurate records were not kept in 1946 and 1947. Simply pieces of paper that have become jumbled all over the place. 'I'll show you.'

The registrar rummaged through filing cabinets behind the counter in the main office, returning with handfuls of loose birth certificates. A dozen or so of these spilled into the floor and were left there.

'There is one individual, a doctor named Dr Mehta, who is currently in Oman but will return next week. I know he has a copy of Freddie's birth certificate.' Despite my best efforts, I was unable to locate Dr Mehta.

My research into the family's history did not go down well with everyone. Perviz's lovely daughter Diana was underwhelmed, stating that she was not interested in 'Freddie Mercouri'. Why?

'He left Zanzibar when I was a kid,' she shrugged, her face flushed. 'He gave away his surname. He did not live like the rest of us. He had nothing to do with us. He never returned. He didn't think much of Zanzibar. He was an unknown. He was from another world.'

She declined to go into further detail. So there was more to it.

Diana's approach was consistent with what I saw elsewhere. Although other Zanzibaris today claim to live in homes originally held by the Bulsara family, none could provide solid proof, and no one appeared to care. 'I don't know anything, and neither does anyone else,' remarked one Indian shopkeeper. Anyone who says they do is merely guessing. These guides, in particular, who accompany you about the island and show you the sights. They only care about money. Nobody knows anything anymore. So many people abruptly left at the same moment, a long time ago. But, if you find out, will you kindly come back here and tell me? Because I'm sick of people constantly asking me. Americans. Americans from the South. English. German. Japanese. Locals do not comprehend. Who was this individual in the first place?'

Who was Zanzibar's most well-known son? This island is the ultimate destination for Queen pilgrims. Specialist tour companies provide expensive fan-friendly vacations to the singer's birthplace, where a few eateries with stunning views and a couple of gift shops profit from the connection. But Freddie was never given star status in his lifetime. There is no Freedom of the City. There is no official archive entry. At the time of my visit to the local museum, there was no mention. There is no old residence that has been transformed into a personal shrine. There is no statue, waxwork, or effigy, no mass-produced ashtray or fridge magnet, not even a postcard carrying his likeness - but postcards of practically everything else exist. Perhaps not even thermometers in this area contain mercury. If there was ever a reason to seek the polar opposite of Elvis Presley's Graceland in Memphis, this is it.

When I returned home, the mystery of the missing birth certificate reared its head once more. Marcela Delorenzi, an Argentinian - that Argentinian - made contact out of nowhere. She informed me she was on her way to London with a surprise for me. The Argentine broadcaster and journalist brought me a copy of Freddie's birth certificate. I hadn't requested it. We'd never spoken before. I hadn't sought to find her because she had asked for nothing in return. If there was any culpability, it was not brought up. She stated that the original handwritten document was still in the Records Office when she received it. She'd noticed it. Perhaps, in the end, it was sold for a large sum of money and is now housed in a private collection somewhere.

The Association for Islamic Mobilisation and Propagation (UAMSHO), a Zanzibar Muslim organisation, objected vehemently against plans to commemorate Freddie's 60th birthday on the island in 2006. The outraged group demanded that a 'gay-tourist' beach party be cancelled, and that thousands of followers travelling from all over the world be sent home, claiming that he had violated Islam with his openly gay, flamboyant lifestyle until his tragic death in 1991 from AIDS.

It was hardly surprising. When Zanzibar officially outlawed homosexual relationships in 2004, LGBT communities around the world were outraged. However, UAMSHO head Abdallah Said Ali warned that the event would "send out the wrong signals."

'We don't want our children to believe that gays are accepted in Zanzibar,' he said. 'We have a religious commitment to safeguard morality in society, and anyone who corrupts Islamic principles must be stopped,' says the author.

Regardless of Islamic principles, there was always the faith of Freddie's own family to consider. He deeply loved and respected his parents and sister. He also understood all too well that orthodox Zoroastrians favour the suppression of homosexuality, which was probably the main reason Freddie battled for so long to suppress his own desires. 'The man who lies with mankind as man lies with womankind, or as a lady lies with mankind, is a Daeva (demon): this guy is a worshipper of the Daevas, a male paramour of the Daevas,' says the sacred Zoroastrian literature the Vendidad.

For the Parsees, homosexuality is not only wicked, but also a kind of devil worship.

Let us put this into context. Consensual homosexual conduct between adults is still prohibited in 70 of the world's 195 countries. Only male-male intercourse is prohibited in 40 of them. Sexual actions between two adult males became lawful in England and Wales in 1967, but not in Scotland until 1980 and Northern Ireland until 1982. Gay rights organizations fought for the age of consent for heterosexuals and gays to be equalized in the 1980s and 1990s. In England, Scotland, Wales, and Northern Ireland, the age of consent is now sixteen.

'Freddie didn't live like the rest of us,' his cousin Diana had said. 'He was from another world.'

The naked truth is preferable to the best-dressed deception. Freddie had obviously abandoned his African nation for the most basic of reasons.

Perhaps he sensed 'hiraeth' in his heart. Its original Welsh meaning cannot be translated into a single word. It expresses melancholy, a deep sadness for what has been lost. Did Freddie, like most of us, subconsciously lament his lost innocence, yearning for chapters of his history he couldn't access?

We return from time to time. We return. We soothe our grownup selves with peaceful reminiscence. Freddie could never do it. He'd constantly have to fill the vacuum somewhere else. Some feel he made peace with his history with the band's first success, 'Seven Seas of Rhye,' in 1974. The lyrics of this hard-rock song on an otherwise progressive album were inspired by a dream realm constructed by young Freddie and his tiny sister Kashmira. Could the secrets of their Persian ancestry, particularly the epic voyage of the prophet Zarathustra, have fuelled their flights of fancy and inspired their Rhye fairytales? According to Phil Swern, a Radio 2 producer, music archivist, and renowned record collector, it is likely.

'From comments he made in interviews over the years, it has always seemed to me that "Seven Seas of Rhye" was about his life in Zanzibar,' Phil explains. 'It was where he escaped to, at least in his imagination. When reality became too much for him, he always had that.'

Freddie defined the song's subject as 'a fabrication of my imagination' in a radio interview.

'Most of my lyrics and songs are fantasies,' he says. 'They're all made up by me. They are not grounded; rather, they are airy-fairy. I'm not one of those authors who walks down the street and is immediately inspired by a vision, nor am I one of those individuals who wants to go on safari to receive inspiration from the wild animals surrounding me, or to go up onto mountain tops or anything like that. No, I can acquire ideas just by sitting in the bath.'

Whatever else happened, Rhye was a recurring theme. Other early Queen songs, such as 'Lily of the Valley,' 'The March of the Black Queen,' and 'My Fairy King,' also included the magical land. Its allure was to prove progressively more far-reaching and long-lasting. The Seven Seas of Rhye is a location in Queen's futuristic jukebox stage musical We Will Rock You, which premiered in London in 2002. The rebel Bohemians are transported there after being brain-wiped by Khashoggi, leader of the Globalsoft police.

As the closing bars of 'Seven Seas of Rhye' fade, an ancient English bucket-and-spade ballad crooned by a noisy saloon bar crowd echoes fleetingly: 'Oh, I do like to be beside the seaside'. Another nod to Freddie's carefree beach days, to the palm-fringed, immaculate coral reefs of his youth?

We have no way of knowing. What we do know is that the man who broke the code of his family's faith could never have been welcomed on the mountain.

# 3. PANCHGANI

I was invited to a cocktail party and VIP preview of the Freddie Mercury Photographic Exhibition at London's Royal Albert Hall in November 1996. It was held to mark the fifth anniversary of his death. From Marje, Freddie's cleaning girl, to Ken Testi, the band's first-ever manager, to Denis O'Regan, a regular Queen photographer, everyone in the room that night had a direct connection to Freddie and Queen. Freddie's elderly parents were also present. They greeted me kindly when I introduced myself. Bomi Bulsara, his father, took my hand in his.

'It's fantastic to see all of these images displayed, and to see so many people here in memory of our dear boy. 'We're quite proud of ourselves,' he remarked.

The show would travel across the world, stopping in places such as Paris, Montreux, and Mumbai. Following the Great Pretender's London debut, a number of other journalists chose to 'out' him for having 'hidden his Indian roots'. Freddie was "exposed" as Britain's first Asian music sensation in headlines such as "Bombay Rhapsody" and "Star of India." Despite the fact that it contained less than a phrase of truth, the yarn generated multiple fantastic page leads. As a result, Freddie's Persian ancestry was called into question. A widespread debate arose. This infuriated London's Persian Parsee community. Nobody on Fleet Street gave a hoot about it.

'Just because our ancestors haven't lived in Persia since the ninth century doesn't make us any less Persian,' said a Parsee community spokeswoman in London.

'While Parsees are referred to as "Indian Zoroastrians," we are actually descendants of Persian Zoroastrians who migrated to India in the seventh and eighth centuries to avoid Muslim persecution. We are not Indian because we immigrated to India. Is it possible to be Jewish if your family has not resided in Palestine for the past two thousand years? There is a significant distinction between race and nationality. Between ancestors and citizenship. The Persian Parsee may not have a place to call home [modern-day Iran was previously their territory]. Nonetheless, he is Persian at heart.'

You only had to look at Freddie to know what he thought. His traditional Persian looks were undeniably at contrast with what is popularly referred to as "Indian." Every image, despite the extra teeth, communicates the story.

Freddie's parents, Bomi and Jer, were both British subjects born in colonial India prior to independence, and their nationality was British-Indian. This was legally recorded, both at the time of their own births and at the birth of their son. Notably, they declared themselves to be Parsees. Freddie was born in Zanzibar and was hence termed Zanzibari. It's possible he was more African than Asian. 'Britain's first Asian pop star' was stretching it: another fresh hook to hang old frames on. Why didn't his family object to this erasure of their history, to this disregard of their precious heritage? Their actions have frequently appeared perplexing.

The Bulsaras were a quiet, conscientious, and homely people who were unmaterialistic and pleased with their lot, moving at their own pace while adhering to their religion and culture's rites, laws, and prohibitions. Both were physically petite and built delicately. In terms of appearance, Freddie was more like his mother, with large lips, an open smile, and unique teeth. Bomi and Jer kept to themselves in public, but were always pleasant and convivial behind closed doors, albeit a touch on the reserved side. Bomi was neither a dominant role model nor macho hero to his kid, despite the fact that they were dutiful family members with a strong sense of tradition and who knew their position. Freddie was more at ease with the matriarchs of the family, and he had no desire to follow in his father's clerical footsteps. While his mother encouraged him to study law, the prospect of working in an office turned him off.

Because the Bulsaras were so reticent and unobtrusive, there was minimal physical contact between them and their children, as Freddie would later relate to his loves Barbara Valentin and Jim Hutton. Sabine, the family's nanny, looked after their children on a daily basis when they were still living in Zanzibar. Neither Freddie nor Kashmira were beaten, but they were never cuddled much either. According to Jim, Freddie used to wonder if his lack of affection as a child was what led to a "disproportionate obsession with physical love in adulthood." ..a desire that all too frequently manifested itself in meaningless sex, because he couldn't have one without the other. Sex was never a substitute for the thing he desired most, affection. ..He had confirmation that he was liked. He was very childish about it. All of the cuddling and stroking he bestowed on the cats, for example, was for himself.'

Freddie - then Farrokh - was enrolled as 'Farookh Bomi Bulsara' (note the spelling change compared to that on his birth certificate) at St Peter's Church of England School in Panchgani, where he was admitted to 'Class Three' on 14 February 1955, when he was only eight years old, according to official school records. He'd be there for a decade, only visiting his folks once a year, for a month each summer. It's no surprise that his connection with his mother and father deteriorated, as seen by the respectful but unfeeling letters he addressed to them. Freddie was expected to keep a stiff upper lip and a brave face, but it is impossible to imagine him not feeling vulnerable and lonely so far away from home, without even the luxury of a phone to call his parents whenever he missed them, which happened frequently.

'He was six when I was born, so I only had a year with him, but I was always aware of my proud bigger brother protecting me,' his sister Kashmira recounted in a November 2000 interview with the Mail on Sunday.

'He didn't always return home for the holidays; sometimes he'd stay with my father's sister in Bombay, or with my mother's sister, and it was she who got him started on the piano and drawing. He was gifted in every way. Of course, it made me sick. All of his school reports were saved by his parents.'

The eight-year-old Freddie's journey from home to his new school was difficult. Freddie's cousin Perviz recounts, "He went by ship with his father before taking the train up to Poona [now Pune]."

'It was a long and exhausting journey. There were regular ships from Zanzibar to Bombay, India's busiest, most industrialised, and most sophisticated city, and we visited there frequently since we had family there. During the school holidays, Freddie would visit my auntie Jer, Bomi's sister. She was a lovely, gentle lady who also looked after the children of another of my father's siblings in India.'

Panchgani ('Five Hills'), a classic British Raj hill station in Western India, is famous for its lovely old bungalows, public buildings, ancient Parsee houses, and rich strawberry fields. During the Raj, the calm colonial town was established as a sanatorium and relaxation resort. It's easy to see why. Its high-altitude, iron-rich waters and dense, volcanic red soil make it a famous tourist destination, with views of coastal lowlands, dense forest, and the River Krishna. Many people travel four or five hours from Mumbai for "Monsoon getaways." They walk, ride, and relax here, away from the dust and heat of the Indian plains. Some parents bring their children to these English-style residential institutions.

St Peter's School still exists today. It was founded in 1904 and continues to encourage tolerance of faiths as different as Catholicism and Zoroastrianism while upholding traditional Indian values and culture. 'Ut Prosim' ('That I may profit') is the school's motto. Its crest, described as a "symbol of hope and rebirth," depicts a phoenix rising from flames, holding an olive branch of peace in its beak. Mr Oswal D. Basin, Freddie's headmaster, arrived in 1947, the year India gained freedom. He was principal until 1974, just when Queen was enjoying the amuse-bouche of stardom. While the school does not brag about its rock 'n' roll ties, it is rarely reluctant to welcome visitors. Employees have even helped with research and filming for Freddie Mercury documentaries. Freddie is one of the school's most prominent Old Boys, along with his classmate and contemporary Victory Rana - subsequently Lt General Victory Rana of the Nepalese Army - and Ravi Punjabi, philanthropist and businessman.

Freddie had been brainwashed into the family faith and was a full-fledged Zoroastrian by the time he arrived on this pleasant, wide fifty-eight-acre campus. He witnessed the Navjote ('Navjote') rite when he was eight years old. This, like Christian Confirmation, includes both girls and boys, while approaching the male Jewish Bar Mitzvah in style more closely. The ritual includes a cleaning bath to represent the purifying of mind and spirit, the wearing of a symbolic white tunic and wool cord, and the recitation of ancient prayers over a sacred and eternal flame. Such fires are central to the Zoroastrian religion. Flames are said to have burnt constantly for thousands of years in some fire temples. The Zend Avesta, or sacred books, have no explicit rules, only the 'Three Good Things' by which Parsees have long attempted to live. 'Humata, Hukhta, Huvarshta' means 'good thoughts, good words, and excellent acts'.

St Peter's was largely regarded as the top boys' public school in Panchgani throughout Freddie's time there. It provided a comprehensive English education leading to Cambridge University O-level and A-level examinations, with consistently good outcomes. Its school year extended from mid-June to mid-April, attracting families from the United States, Canada, and the Gulf, as well as from all throughout India. The primary eight-week holiday fell between April and June, with an additional fortnight off at Christmas, with allowances to India's environment. St Peter's had strong discipline and harsh living conditions. On Wednesdays and Saturday lunchtimes, there was hot water for baths, but the rest of the week was freezing. Matron oversaw bathing rituals while also running the school hospital with the support of a resident nurse and on-call doctor. While boys of different faiths attended the school and their faiths were respected, Sunday Mass was mandatory for all. No student was permitted to leave campus unless escorted by a member of staff. For all of this, St Peter's was well-known as a loving institution with a peaceful and joyful family culture that encouraged students' abilities to bring out the best in them. Whatever his feelings were at the time, Freddie subsequently stated that he felt privileged to have been sent there, given his parents' sacrifices.

Not only was it difficult to pay the school tuition - Freddie's father was a low-paid government clerk with little money to spare - but it was also difficult for Bomi and Jer to part with their only son, and for his sister to be separated from her only sibling.

That sense of luxury was insufficient to alleviate separation anxiety. Being sent thousands of miles away to school at such a young age must have been a horrible wrench for him, having grown extraordinarily close to his mother and sister Kashmira as a small boy. It's difficult to imagine Freddie feeling anything other than lonely and terrified as he tucked himself in at night, wishing for a cuddle and a bedtime story. Those who knew him subsequently said Freddie harboured a deep anger against his parents for "sending him away," despite the fact that he was always a respectable and kind adult son. He certainly made every effort to overcome his sentiments of rejection.

Jer and Bomi must have felt they were acting correctly at the time. Giving their son the finest possible start in life surely resulted in financial difficulties. But sending a shy little boy like Freddie to school so far away was possibly their biggest blunder. Some young children appear to handle prolonged separation from their family better than others. That wrench, at just eight years old, was first unbearable for Freddie, a sensitive boy who, by his own admission, was a touch clingy. In his cramped dormitory bed, surrounded by nineteen other new lads, he would weep himself to sleep at night. Freddie's outlook and expectations unavoidably changed when he was denied daily one-on-one care and attention at the most critical period of his development and at a very impressionable age.

He'd seek solace in the company of like-minded young men. Along with Victory Rana, he befriended Derrick Branche, who eventually migrated to Australia to pursue a career as an actor. In 1985, just as Freddie was stealing the show at Live Aid, Branche appeared in My Beautiful Laundrette, a comedic drama starring Daniel Day-Lewis that investigated interactions between White and Asian populations and addressed, poignantly, problems like homosexuality and racism.

Farang Irani, who later became a restaurant in Bombay, and Bruce Murray, who was last seen working as a porter at London's Victoria railway station, were also among Freddie's group. These five guys would become inseparable over the next few years, sleeping close to one another in their dormitory and collaborating on innumerable schoolboy pranks. Freddie was packed off to either his paternal aunt

Her or his maternal aunt Sheroo during term and half-term breaks, and he was rarely reunited with his parents, even during school holidays.

'You had to do what you were instructed, so the most logical thing to do was to make the most of it,' Freddie explained years later. 'I learned to take care of myself and grew up swiftly.'

So began the shaping of the real' Freddie's personality, which would last until the end of his life.

The realisation that he would have to stand up to the school bullies presented a difficult learning curve for Freddie. It also occurred to him that the name would have to be changed. 'Farrokh' was a mouthful, pronounced the Persian way: 'Farroch', as in 'loch', as opposed to the African 'Farouk'. He was relieved when teachers and acquaintances called him by the diminutive of a proper English name. 'Freddie,' he was nicknamed. Fortunately, it stuck. His parents and family made no concerns, and he is still referred to as 'Freddie' to this day. The change in surname would occur long later, for several reasons.

When Freddie was approximately ten years old, he developed an aloof, condescending demeanour that he would have for the rest of his life. While he might be a jerk at times, he was never cruel or malevolent.

He wasn't your normal team guy. He excelled at solo and one-on-one sports like chess, sprinting, boxing, and table tennis. He won the school table tennis championship before the age of eleven. While rugby and football were not his interests, he was believed to prefer cricket, though he later disputed this. Who knows if he thought an open love of the game would undermine his hard-rock image. He won the Junior All-Rounder award in 1958, when he was about twelve years old, and the Academic Prowess award the following year. He played the lead in several plays and sang a solo in the Seniors' production of "The Indian Love Call." Art was his favourite subject. He spent a lot of his free time drawing and painting, especially for his aunt Sheroo and grandparents in Bombay. He also began to pursue extracurricular music with zeal.

Even in the late 1950s and early 1960s, Bombay had a cosmopolitan East-meets-West culture that allowed Western pop and rock to flourish. While Freddie enjoyed the classical music he studied, especially opera, he preferred contemporary music even more. He began playing the piano and joined the choir, completing exams up to and including Grade IV in both Theory and Practical. He formed his first band, The Hectics, with close pals. Freddie quickly became the talk of the town thanks to his vibrant boogie-woogie piano playing style. The Hectics first appeared in school concerts and the annual fete. Local schoolgirls would scream their lungs out in the front, having learned that this was the proper way to behave in front of a group. Pop icons of the time included Elvis Presley, Cliff Richard, Fats Domino, and Little Richard, and Freddie took inspiration from them. He worked hard to imitate their styles. He wasn't ready for the stage, so he let his friend Bruce Murray, who played guitar and sang lead vocals, take the lead.

'Of course, there was a school choir, which sang all the traditional choral works and hymns, and which practised on a regular basis in order to lead the singing at the school's church services,' recalled Freddie's former schoolmate and Hectics bandmate Derrick Branche.

'The chorus had about twenty-five members, and we were frequently intermingled with girls from one of the town's sister schools. Not only did Freddie enjoy the choir, but I believe he had feelings for one of the ladies, Gita Bharucha, who was fifteen at the time.'

Although it has been reported that Freddie was sexually active at St Peter's from around the age of fourteen, and that his interactions were primarily with other boys and a couple of paid school hands, Freddie's first-ever girlfriend is sceptical.

'I never assumed Bucky was gay,' Gita explained. I never saw any proof of that. Perhaps his masters were aware and kept quiet. We, his buddies, were completely unaware. He was a flashy entertainer who was completely at ease on stage. He was always cast as a girl in plays!'

Gita was difficult to find once she married, changed her name to Choksi, and relocated to Frankfurt to work for an Indian tour operator. She was first hesitant to talk about Freddie when I found her. She finally consented, and we met in London.

'I met Freddie for the first time in 1955, when I enrolled at the Kimmins School in Panchgani,' she explained.

'It was run by English Protestant missionaries. I moved out in 1963. We were buddies for the majority of Freddie's 10 years in "Panchi." I was from Bombay, but I lived in Panchi with my mother and grandparents. I was a day student. The boys from St Peter's would attend the Kimmins kindergarten before continuing on to Standard Three at St Peter's proper. For years, a bunch of us had been in the same class. Victory Rana and I were best friends throughout high school. And Bucky - we used to call Freddie that because of his teeth. Another was Derrick Branche.

'Bucky and I were close friends, but not unusually close. Nothing personal. All we're doing is holding hands. We used to go riding by renting bicycles for three rupees per day. We'd also go out on Mahabaleshwar Lake in rowing boats. Mum would let me have a party or invite a few friends around for lunch, and then we'd go on walks or play games. Bucky frequently visited our home throughout the holidays. He was incredibly kind and courteous. My mother and grandmother both adored him.'

Janet Smith, a Panchgani school mistress who resided at St Peter's while Freddie was there because her mother taught him Art, was certain of Freddie's homosexuality.

'He had this strange habit of addressing people as "Darling," which seemed a little fey. I just knew he was gay since he was here. It was odd in those days, to be sure, but it was almost expected in a boy like Freddie. Normally, it would have been horrifying. But it wasn't the case with Freddie. It was fine. It wasn't just a phase; it was a basic part of him. I couldn't help but feel terrible for him, knowing that the others would mock him. The strange thing was, he didn't appear to mind.'

Gita Bharucha and Freddie had been inseparable, but she never heard from him again after he departed Panchgani.

'I know it was very sad, but that was it. As if he wants to move on from his life in India to the next stage.'

Freddie's grades had begun to fall by the time he entered Class Ten. He failed the end-of-year exam and dropped out of school before year eleven. Freddie never completed his O-levels. He lost interest in his studies and focused his sights on more glamorous aspirations, possibly due to confusion about his sexuality and the more creative pursuits of Music and Art. Previous biographies state that he graduated from St Peter's with a string of O-levels with exceptional grades in English Language, History, and Art, however he did not. When put against the remarkable scholastic achievements of his other band members, it becomes evident why the facts were skewed by early publicists. Brian May earned a BSc Hons in Physics after studying Physics and Math at Imperial College London. He would finish his PhD in Astrophysics thirty years later. John Deacon earned a first-class Honours degree in Electronics at Chelsea College, which is now part of King's College London, while Roger Taylor was accepted to the London Hospital Medical College to study Dentistry before dropping out to pursue music.

'Freddie didn't want to seem as a. ..'He was a dimwit in comparison to the other members of Queen who had accomplished so much,' said Jim Jenkins, official Queen biographer and co-author of As It Began. Perhaps that's why he claimed to have passed his O-levels when he hadn't. In the circumstances, it's understandable.'

Sheroo Khory, Freddie's maternal aunt, spoke to me about her loving nephew from her home in Bombay's Dadar Parsee colony. Bombay was renamed Mumbai in 1995 as the former name was judged an unwelcome remnant of British colonial authority.

'Even when Freddie stayed with Jer, he would always return to me after breakfast and spend entire days with me. I encouraged him because he was quite excellent at drawing. He created an exquisite image of two horses in a storm when he was eight years old, which he signed "Farrokh." It was once hung in his mother's home. I'm not sure if she still has it.'

'That was it,' she remarked after Freddie arrived in England. 'He never wanted to return to India. He identified as British, admired the more civilised way of life there, and, most importantly, admired the judicial system - especially in comparison to all the corruption in India. But he did keep in touch with me on a regular basis. He also provided me money for an eye operation that I really needed and wanted to take me on a European vacation. He never forgot his grandmother.'

Years later, Sheroo stated, she began corresponding with her nephew's old girlfriend Mary Austin on a regular basis, exchanging images of Freddie as a child and Freddie the famous rock singer. She also mentioned Freddie's 'enemies' in England and how she used to worry about his safety. Religion, she added, bothered her, especially rumours that Freddie had converted to Christianity just before his death.

'This news devastated the entire family,' she explained.

'It was a huge blow. We were all tired of hearing so many awful things about dear Freddie, especially the lies about him becoming a Christian. Which I am certain he did not. 'Not to my knowledge, and I'm confident I would have known.'

Despite popular belief, Freddie returned to Zanzibar in 1963 to finish his secondary education at the Roman Catholic St Joseph's Convent School. At this school, Freddie was well known by Bonzo Fernandez, a former Zanzibar police officer who eventually served as a cab driver.

'I recall him having a nice relationship with his family and a good sister. Freddie had a good upbringing. They were pleasant and polite folks. We used to get together and play hockey and cricket. 'He was particularly talented at cricket,' he claimed.

'I knew he'd been gone at school in India, but he never talked about his time there. We used to jump out the window after school and swim in the sea, which Freddie loved to do. We used to swim at the Starhe Club on Shangani Street, which had a beautiful beach. We'd pedal to Fumba in the south, Mangapwani in the northwest, the location of the old slave caverns, or Chwaka on the peninsula's far southeastern tip. We would sometimes go as a group. We'd go swimming, have snacks, and climb coconut trees. We were a little mischievous, but not too horrible. There will be no alcohol, drugs, or smoke in our day.

'I can still see that thin and cheerful little lad in his short blue pants and white shirt. He was always well-dressed, particularly for cricket, where his spotless whites seemed whiter than everyone else's.

'After the Revolution, we all left the island. I never found out where Freddie went or what happened to him. I only found out later that we were both in the UK at the same time. My old classmate and close friend had become that world-famous rock singer only after his death.'

Gita Choksi had a similar experience.

'Years later, when I discovered who he had become, I bought some of his albums and thoroughly appreciated his music,' she recalled.

'However, I never saw him play live. That has always been a source of disappointment for me. Another of our dear school friends went to a Queen performance once and tried to get backstage to see Bucky. But when he finally got a good look at him, Freddie just looked right through him and said, "I'm sorry, but I'm afraid I just don't know who you are."

'That was when we all knew he didn't want anything to do with us anymore. He was resolved to leave the past behind him.'

# 4. LONDON

The 1950s saw a significant increase in nationalist resistance to British rule. The loss of India and Pakistan by Britain in 1947, the independence of Burma and Ceylon in 1948, and China's social revolution in 1949 all had a significant impact on nationalist struggles in North, Northeast, and East Africa. Zanzibar was not spared. In order to achieve change, trade unions have begun to redefine themselves as political parties. The Zanzibar National Party, created in 1956 by minority Arabs and Shirazi, was superseded by the Afro-Shirazi Party, led primarily by African mainlanders. Strikes were crippling numerous businesses, and labour militancy was on the rise. Pro-Arab election results, combined with disappointingly low clove and coconut harvests, sparked riots. Although independence was secured in December 1963, electoral representation disparities incensed the black African majority, resulting in a radical left-wing rebellion. The new Sultan Jamshid bin Abdulla was toppled in the violent Zanzibar Revolution of 1964, and Sheikh Abeid Amani Karume, President of the Afro-Shirazi Party, was installed as the first President of Zanzibar. In brutal street fighting, thousands were slain. The Bulsaras, like many others, fled for their lives. Freddie's family left Zanzibar with only a few pieces of luggage, heading for England, where relatives had offered them asylum. They didn't look back.

'That was the end of our family bond,' Freddie's cousin Perviz recalls with sadness.

'When I found out later that Freddie had become a famous musician, I was overjoyed that we had such a genius in the family. We were so proud of him. But he didn't say anything to any of us. He didn't even send us a tape.'

Following the Revolution, Zanzibar and Tanganyika formed a union in April 1964, with Zanzibar remaining semi-autonomous under the new name Tanzania. Zanzibaris nowadays are a relaxed, calm, and accepting people, with the exception of their almost universal dislike of homosexuality.

When the Bulsaras landed at Feltham, in the London Borough of Hounslow, a nondescript town about thirteen miles southwest of London and a couple of miles from Heathrow Airport, they were unprepared for the culture shock.

'My father had a British passport,' Kashmira explained,'so it seemed like the natural choice to come to England.'

'Freddie was very happy,' his mother, Jer, said. '"England is the place we should go, Mum," he added. 'But it was incredibly difficult,' she says.

The dreary, grey orderliness of flight-path suburbia, much alone the chilly environment, was a dramatic contrast to their experiences in Zanzibar and Bombay. They arrived in London with no rank, money, servants, or mansion. Despite his government ties and track record, Freddie's father received no formal accounting employment. Bomi soon found work as a cashier for the Forte catering firm, while his mother became an assistant at a local Marks & Spencer. Even when her son became famous, mom continued to work.

'I was struck by how conspicuous we were,' Kash, who was about twelve years old at the time, recalled.

'Freddie was quite concerned with his appearance. Everyone else had their hair long and untidy, while he looked neat and tidy with his hair combed back. I used to stroll behind him so that no one would assume I was with him.

'But he changed his appearance swiftly,' she continued. 'He used to spend hours in front of the mirror grooming his hair.'

Freddie was eighteen when he found himself in a quandary. Despite his desire to fly, he was still financially dependent on his parents and hence had to stay at home. Despite being well informed of everything the city has to offer, being confined under their roof restricted his manners.

'People in small communities find it difficult to accept anything or anyone that deviates from the standard,' says James Saez, producer, writer, multi-instrumentalist, and former engineer at Los Angeles' Record Plant.

'West Virginia has a lot of Jesus and weapons. Growing up in Zanzibar and India, Freddie was well aware of this. You have to get to the city if you come from such places and are this whole different person within who may not find acceptance. Freddie was fortunate to have had to relocate to London at that time.'

While many of his peers were now earning their own money and having independent lives, Freddie's parents wanted him to continue his schooling. However, their son will not pursue a profession in law or accounting. Freddie said that he was 'not intelligent enough' for academic pursuits. Instead, he attended Isleworth College in 1966 to get an A level in Art before transferring to Ealing College of Art the following year to begin a course in Graphic Design and Illustration. He graduated with a Diploma in Graphic Art and Design in the summer of 1969, at the age of twenty-three. Far from being "the equivalent of a degree," it fell short of matching the scholastic genius of his future bandmates.

'I went to art school with the goal of receiving my diploma, which I accomplished, and then becoming an artist - intending to earn my keep as a freelancer,' Freddie explained.

'He'd go out a lot, too, and stay out all night,' Kashmira recalled. My mother and he used to argue about it all the time. And mother was continuously harping on him about getting a degree, but he was adamant about doing what he wanted. There was a lot of slamming of doors. Mum was overjoyed when Freddie succeeded.

'I actually got to know him only at this time,' she added. 'He'd help me with my homework, and I'd pose for him while he was drawing.'

Freddie worked in the catering department at Heathrow Airport and in a container warehouse on the Feltham commercial estate during his college breaks. He countered jibes from his coworkers, who ridiculed him for his 'feminine hands and camp, showy ways,' that he was actually a musician marking time.

London, the Mecca of teenage culture, was in full swing by this point. With the pop boom coming to an end, the singles market began to wane in favour of LPs. Ballroom managers began converting to straight dancing sessions after discovering that rock 'n' roll 'beat' evenings were no longer popular. The Beatles remained the most popular group in the world, despite opposition from The Rolling Stones, The Animals, Manfred Mann, and Georgie Fame on the charts. Tom Jones, a muscular vocalist from the Welsh valleys, was the most recent pop sensation. Sandie Shaw and Petula Clark were Britain's most popular female singers, and the previous year's folk craze was on the rise. Joan Baez and Bob Dylan both issued political statements regarding Vietnam. Dylan was befriended by

Donovan. In the British hit parade, Elvis Presley, Peter, Paul, and Mary, The Byrds, The Righteous Brothers, Sonny and Cher, and other Americans held their own. Television was gaining traction, with Cathy McGowan on Ready, Steady, Go! dominating pop programming.

Fashion was also thriving. Mary Quant and Angela Cash commanded the design scene, while John Stephen became known as the "King of Carnaby Street," which was the Mod capital of the globe at the time. Young fashion had developed its own distinct voice. Wearing T-shirts emblazoned with bull's-eyes and Union Jacks, The Who popularised 'Op Art' designs. John Lennon popularised the tweed peaked cap, while Dave Clark, of The Dave Clark Five and later a close friend of Freddie's, popularised white Levi trousers. Freddie, who was slim and snake-hipped, preferred crushed velvet and corduroy hipster pants. The outfit was completed with leather and suede coats, satin, silk, and floral blouses, and ankle boots.

Living on the outskirts of the most exciting city in the world made Freddie restless and rebellious. He longed more than ever that he could afford to leave home, and soon began dosing on the floors of pals.

'Fred lived like a gypsy,' Brian May said.

He wanted everything, and he wanted it now, just outside his door: fashion boutiques, record stores and booksellers, music venues, bars, and clubs. Kensington Market and the famed Biba shop will soon become his haunts.

Ealing College of Art had several prominent alumni, including Pete Townshend of The Who and Ronnie Wood of The Faces, who subsequently became a Rolling Stone. Former student Jerry Hibbert recalls the college as both modern and practical, producing graduates who were ready for the industry. He started two years behind Freddie, having arrived from Oxford, and got to know him well through mutual musical interests.

'Ealing College was going through a lot of changes at the time,' Jerry recalls.

'The major issue was New York's advertising district, Madison Avenue. It had an impact on our way of life, right down to how we dressed. We wanted to look like New York advertising executives. We shaved our heads and arrived at college with suits and ties since hippies were everywhere and art students like to stand out. Everything was very stylized. We even had an issue with the way we walked. We were not your typical Union Bar students, all rugby players and beer drinkers. The college cafeteria served as our social hub and meeting spot. Freddie - he was still Freddie Bulsara back then - used to hang out with us all there. He was certainly into fashion and clothing. He was always aware of his appearance.'

'Art school makes you more fashion savvy,' Freddie would later say. 'I'm always one step ahead.'

Freddie quickly lost interest in his studies due to boredom with course work and a lack of discipline and diligence. However, he relished the more hedonistic aspects of college life. During class, he spent the most of his time sketching portraits of his classmates and his new idol, Jimi Hendrix, whose influence changed Freddie's life. Chas Chandler, The Animals' bass player, had discovered the African American from Seattle, who was only four years Freddie's senior, in New York. Chandler rapidly established a big following for The Jimi Hendrix Experience, which also included drummer Mitch Mitchell and bass player Noel Redding, by persuading The Beatles, Pete Townshend, and Eric Clapton to turn up at the 'in' clubs to witness his insanely brilliant protégé play. The American rendered his opponents stunned. Hendrix displayed a dazzling range of methods while playing his white Fender Stratocaster upside down, behind his neck, and with his teeth, manoeuvres he'd picked up from a string of unnamed musicians. Although many later rock guitarists took the instrument in new directions, few could match Hendrix's brilliance.

'Jimi Hendrix was really a handsome man, a superb showman, and a passionate musician,' said Freddie later.

'I would go across the nation to see him whenever he played because he had everything a rock 'n' roll star should have: style and presence. He didn't need to push anything. He'd just walk in, and the entire place would be on fire. He embodied everything I wished to be.'

Freddie's ambition became clear. While he was still enthralled by the musicians who had inspired him in school - Cliff Richard, Elvis Presley, Little Richard, and Fats Domino - Hendrix blew him away, and he set about recreating himself in the image of the American rocker. Freddie's future composition, arranging, and vocal techniques must challenge traditional expectations, much as Jimi's guitar work did. They were left gaping in the aisles by Hendrix's stage presence and flamboyant manner. Freddie knew he had to follow suit. Hendrix was radically unique, performed in novel ways, and was so exuberant that his audiences were weary. Freddie vowed to one day have the same effect on his own fans. Hendrix could make any music, no matter how boring, sound like it was his own original masterpiece. In 1986, I saw Freddie perform the same thing live on stage in Budapest, bringing tears to the eyes of millions with his version of a simple Hungarian folk melody. He couldn't have cared less about the foreign lyrics scribbled on his hand. The tune had nothing in common with a rock song. But Freddie said it as if he truly meant it. The audience was enthralled.

Back in Kensington, with the drab walls of his little home plastered with photos of his idol, Freddie worked tirelessly to perfect the Hendrix style. Floral jackets in bright colours worn over black or multicoloured shirts, slim slacks, Chelsea boots, chiffon scarves knotted at the Adam's apple, and big silver rings. 'What he wore was no different than what we were all wearing at the time,' said fellow student Graham Rose. Freddie was generally a quiet man, yet he was prone to bouts of laughter. When that happened, he'd put his palm over his mouth to conceal his massive teeth. I recall him as a fantastic guy, really sweet and considerate. He didn't have a vicious streak in him. Many of us were overjoyed when he went on to become such a huge success.'

Freddie did not stand out in college, according to Jerry Hibbert.

'Except for the fact that he loved to sing. He used to sing while sitting at his desk. He was in the room next to mine and a year or two above. He sat next to Tim Staffell, and the two of them used to sing in unison. That was odd, because we were all into blues at the time. Pre-Cream, John Mayall and Eric Clapton. We were preoccupied with all of the underlying forces. For example, we were no longer interested in hearing Eric Clapton do 'Hideaway,' but rather in hearing Freddie King perform it. Freddie Bulsara, like the rest of us, was clearly interested in all of this. As a result, sitting in class singing harmonies made him appear a little crazy. It didn't match what everyone else was doing. That didn't seem to concern either him or Tim. They'd be sitting there working and singing together.'

'Music was always a sideline, and that sort of grew,' Freddie later commented.

'By the time I finished the illustrating course, I was sick of it. I'd had it up to this point. I thought, I don't think I can make a profession out of this because my mind wasn't on it. So I decided to experiment with the music side of things for a time. Everyone wants to be a celebrity, so I reasoned that if I could try, why not?'

In terms of Freddie's personality, Jerry dismisses the notion that he was an attention seeker.

'No, he wasn't that way. He was the sweetest person I'd ever met. I had no idea he was gay, either. He gave no indication of this. He was pleasant and calm. Always courteous and considerate. Your mother would describe him as "well brought-up." He used to play about and sing, pretending to use a ruler as a microphone, but it was all for fun.'

After both had graduated from college, Freddie disregarded his normal rule of avoiding contacting those who had moved on from a period in his life. He and Jerry remained buddies for quite some time.

'It was due to the music,' Jerry says. 'I used to play blues in college, parties, and people's houses. Freddie would come down and join in on the fun. This was before people started playing records at parties. You'd get a band in if you wanted music.'

Freddie soon told Jerry about his desire to pursue a career in music.

'I was in a band for approximately two years after Freddie graduated from college. He came by one day and informed me that he was going to focus on forming a band. "Don't do it, stick to graphics," I warned him. Music is not profitable. 'Stay with what you know.'

Freddie, on the other hand, had made up his mind.

'I did see him after that - I bought or sold him some equipment, I can't recall which. He returned to college to play with a band named Wreckage. To be honest, I didn't think much of them. We just lost touch after that.'

Jerry got into animation, becoming a member of one of the several teams that worked on The Beatles' full-length film, Yellow Submarine.

'I lost interest in music altogether,' he says. 'I discovered that I despised everything. Never bought a record and never saw a band live. Four years later, I heard a DJ on the radio raving about the band Queen. Their first success was "Seven Seas of Rhye." Not too shabby. But I didn't relate the name Freddie Mercury with my Ealing College classmate Freddie Bulsara. Suddenly, there was a lot of attention. He was impossible to overlook. I was strolling past a newsstand one day when I noticed his portrait on the top page of Melody Maker. A large image with a catchy headline. I looked at it and thought to myself, "Bloody hell, that's Freddie Bulsara."

Jerry would subsequently collaborate on a project for Queen near the end of Freddie's life, but he would never see his college friend again.


## 5. QUEEN

When Freddie and fellow college crooner Tim Staffell began hanging out with another student, Nigel Foster, the two-part classroom harmonies had progressed to three-part. Spending most of their spare time developing versions of Jimi Hendrix's British Top Ten successes 'Hey Joe,' 'Purple Haze,' and 'The Wind Cries Mary,' these secret jam sessions, done purportedly for their own enjoyment, would eventually bring them to the attention of the boys who would become Queen.

Tim and Freddie were inseparable for a time. Tim and his fellow college students had only a hazy understanding of Freddie's origins and the circumstances that had brought the Bulsaras to England.

Because Freddie never brought friends home, they got the sense that his parents were distant and unable to integrate or adjust. It was even rumoured, incorrectly, that they barely knew English and were determined to maintain their culture, religion, and language apart. In truth, Freddie had been speaking English since he was a toddler.

Tim was now routinely performing with a semi-professional band called Smile. Freddie began accompanying me to rehearsals. Brian May, a gangly Physics, Maths, and Astronomy student at prestigious Imperial College, was Smile's lead guitarist. Unbeknownst to either of them, he and Freddie had grown up in Feltham in a modest home similar to Freddie's, just a few streets from the Bulsaras' house on Gladstone Avenue. Brian, an academic only kid, had been playing guitar since he was six years old. While still in school, he made his own Red Special guitar from a discarded mahogany fireplace and some oak cuts with the help of his father Harold. He used silver sixpence coins instead of the traditional plectrum. Later, the guitar would accompany him all around the world.

Like Freddie, Brian had dabbled in amateur bands with schoolmates.

'None of the groups got very far since we never played any genuine gigs or took it seriously,' Brian explained.

Tim Staffell, a lad from their school, was singing and humming on a harmonica at a neighbourhood dance one evening when he and his friends noticed him. They asked him to join their band, and he headlined '1984' at their first official show in Twickenham's St Mary's Church Hall. They were hired as Jimi Hendrix's support act at an Imperial College gig in May 1967, demonstrating tremendous promise. They won a tournament at Croydon's Top Rank Club a few months later. A professional career appeared to be in the works.

'1984 was just an amateur band, created at school, although at the end we might have gotten fifteen quid or something,' Brian would later recall.

'We never really played anything substantial in the way of original material - it was a bizarre blend of cover versions, all the stuff that people wanted to hear at the time,' says the band's manager. This was around the time the Stones were breaking out, and we later did Stones and Yardbirds stuff. ..It never made me happy. I quit because I wanted to pursue something where we could create our own content.'

Brian withdrew from the band and the band disbanded after explaining to his bandmates that his education must come first. Brian and Tim Staffell, now Freddie's student and cohort at Ealing College of Art, stayed in touch. They were soon contemplating the mechanics of forming another band, suffering from musical withdrawal. They agreed to try again with Chris Smith, another Ealing undergraduate who was also a good keyboard player, with Smith on organ, Staffell on lead vocals and bass, and May on lead guitar. The drummer was the only thing missing.

Roger Meddows Taylor was almost too gorgeous to be a man, with his baby-blonde hair and deep blue eyes. Taylor, who was born in Norfolk but reared in Truro, had already established himself as a drummer in Cornwall with a band named Johnny Quale and The Reaction. The trio finished fourth in the local Rock and Rhythm Championship and quickly gained a following on the Cornwall circuit. Taylor was voted lead vocalist after Quale left the band. After shortening their name to The Reaction, their fame grew with a musical style mostly centred on soul until they discovered The Jimi Hendrix Experience in 1967. That autumn, Roger moved to London to complete his Dentistry degree at the London Hospital Medical School. He quickly became the fourth flatmate in Shepherd's Bush, where his buddy Les Brown from Truro already lived. Les was a year older than Brian May and attended Imperial College. Roger was now hooked on the goal of being a rock star, but he needed to find a new band to replace his old bandmates in The Reaction, with whom he would re-engage for a few ad hoc gigs during the summer break in 1968. Despite his Don Juan persona, he was shy, personable, and popular with other guys. Eventually, with Les Brown on his side, a chance occurred at the start of the autumn semester. Les discovered a postcard advertising for a 'Ginger Baker/Mitch Mitchell-type drummer' while searching the Imperial College noticeboard for something that could suit his pal. This demonstrated Brian and Tim's seriousness: Baker had built a cult following with the Graham Bond

Organisation, musicians' group' who had recorded with The Who before defecting to Eric Clapton's Cream. Mitchell was a member of The Jimi Hendrix Experience.

The contact name on the card was Brian May's. Roger called him right away. Brian and Tim explained what they were searching for, and soon they were driving over to Roger's flat for a jam session on acoustic guitars and bongos, because Taylor's full drum equipment was still at home in Cornwall, gathering dust. Shortly after, the trio began serious rehearsals in Imperial College's jazz club room. Brian and Tim were not only doing credible versions of other musicians, but they were also writing their own tunes. This early music was more metal than minstrel, with classical overtones and borrowed from an incredible diversity of inspirations. Smile's music was half Elizabethan troubadour, part monster rock, with dramatic drumming, aggressive guitars, strong lead vocals, and sophisticated harmonies, while their lyrics pilfer the works. The whole effect was layered, ornate, and stunning. It was nothing if not a foreshadowing of things to come.

This was the Queen's genuine beginning.

'I could play you Smile tapes that have the same general structures as what we're doing now,' Brian said in a 1977 interview.

Queen synergy was already being established by extremely distinct personalities who beautifully complimented one other. Brian, the nice and quiet type away from the stage, was tall, lean, and angular. His wild dark curls flowed sexily into his eyes as he played, making him irresistibly snake-hipped in his velvet loons. Tim was more rough and ready, and not really fashionable in his ripped denims. Neither was Chris, the group's only member who was studying privately for a Music degree on the side. Blond Roger, who was described as "a drummer both by name and by nature" and "sex on legs," was far too attractive for his own good. The band was propelled by his energy, excitement, always positive, and cleverly hilarious attitude. Those were carefree, hopeful days.

"Are they going to make it?" Brian May's mother and I would ask each other.'", Jer, Freddie's mother, recalled.

Brian received his BSc Honours degree in October 1968, with the diploma given by Her Majesty the Queen Mother in the Royal Albert Hall. He had previously decided to remain at Imperial College as a post-graduate tutor while working on his PhD thesis on the migration of interplanetary dust, with the long-term goal of becoming an astronomer. There was another reason for staying at Imperial: it made gigs and rehearsals easier. Chris Smith and Tim Staffell were still at Ealing. Meanwhile, Roger dropped out of medical school after only finishing half of his degree. The boys supported Pink Floyd at Imperial College just two days after Brian's graduation ceremony, which is both recognized and disputed as Smile's debut gig. They would later open for T. Yes, Rex, and Family. Smile asked Chris Smith to leave the group in February 1969, which Smith disputed, claiming that he had decided to depart due to musical disagreements. The remaining members took their places in their debut charity line-up at the Royal Albert Hall a few nights later. The late DJ John Peel hosted a fundraiser event for the National Council for the Unmarried Mother and Her Child. Brian and Roger had no idea that thirty-five years later, they would be collaborating with Free's lead singer Paul Rodgers (who in the meantime would front Bad Company, The Firm, and The Law) on two acclaimed world tours, on The Cosmos Rocks - Queen's first studio album in nearly fifteen years - and on a live album and two live DVDs.

Tim arrived at a Smile rehearsal in early 1969, accompanied by his art college classmate Freddie Bulsara. The attraction was both immediate and reciprocal. Freddie was at home among competent and seasoned musicians. He was more persuaded than ever that this was how he wanted to spend his life. Brian and Roger were equally captivated by Freddie's appearance, dry humour, and cutting wit.

'I don't think I've ever met someone so ridiculous since,' Roger's pal Les Brown subsequently recalled. He was overjoyed about everything. He once hauled me into a room and forced me to listen to a soul record he particularly enjoyed. At the time, no one acknowledged enjoying the soul; it was all rock. I assume he was displaying his Catholicism.'

Freddie became a regular sight at Smile shows, making open

suggestions about how they should style themselves, passing comments about their performance, and even starting directing them how to sit, stand, walk, and talk.

'He made ideas that couldn't be denied,' Brian recalled. 'At the time, he hadn't done much singing, and we didn't realise he could. We assumed he was just a showy rock musician.'

Freddie graduated from Ealing College in the summer of 1969 without a full-time job. He had no intention of obtaining one. He and Roger Taylor (who had by now ditched the middle name 'Meddows') would manage a tiny ten-pound-a-week 'Kasbah' stand within three-storey Kensington Market, on the antiques selling alley known as 'Death Row'. The majority of the stallholders were colourful, unemployed artists and writers. Michael Caine, Julie Christie, and Norman Wisdom were among their clients. To begin, they sold Freddie's artwork, primarily fashion sketches and paintings of Jimi Hendrix, as well as the work of fellow Ealing College students. They even sold Hendrix Freddie's college thesis. Although all of this is certainly worth thousands of dollars today, none of it was valuable at the time. They needed to increase their earnings. They opted to market fashion since they were unashamed clothing horses. Everything from exotic scarves and cloaks to coats and fur stoles became their stock in trade, all of which was little more than tarty kitsch and jumble sale junk, marketed at brazenly inflated costs. They even started having clothes built up out of old fabrics and trimmings, and became excellent at getting 'work lots'. They bought a crate of moth-eaten fur coats for £50 from a rag seller in Battersea and sold them for £8 each.

'Roger and I go poncing and ultra blagging pretty much everywhere, and lately we've been dubbed a pair of queens,' Freddie wrote to student friend Celine Daley at the time.

Roger and Freddie relished their narcissistic 'Del-Boy-esque' market-trader persona, according to Tim Staffell.

'They loved being obnoxious,' he said. 'Freddie developed his camp side, which he saw as a humorous aspect of his personality. It was never implied that he was gay. He was never sexually explicit.'

Smile had begun to travel with Freddie, who was now an accepted member of their entourage.

The band performed at London's Revolution Club in April 1969, where they met the late Lou Reizner, chairman of Mercury Records' European branch. Lou arranged David Bowie's American deal and went on to become famous for producing Rod Stewart's first two solo albums. He also orchestrated The Who's rock opera Tommy and Rick Wakeman's Journey to the Center of the Earth. He, a Chicago-born former vocalist, offered Smile a one-single deal for the United States alone, which they signed on the spot. Nothing happened until June, when Smile was booked into Soho's Trident Studios.

It was an auspicious start. Normal Sheffield, former drummer with Sixties band The Hunters, and his brother Barry founded Trident Studios in 17 St Anne's Court, a Soho alleyway in the heart of London's West End. The Sheffield brothers"relaxed attitude toward audio-engineering' and the facilities' cutting-edge recording technology drew many prominent .artists. Engineers at other facilities, such as EMI's Abbey Road Studios, continued to work in white coats. Another, not inconsiderable Trident attraction was its already legendary Bechstein piano, upon which Rick Wakeman had laboured tenderly for many a session, and the keys of which still resonated with the notes of Paul McCartney's 'Hey Jude'.

The studios' first huge hit, using the most modern equipment available at the time, was Manfred Mann's 'My Name Is Jack' in March of the previous year. Among the many beloved albums recorded at Trident is Lou Reed's Transformer, which was produced by David Bowie, who also recorded his own masterpieces there, including The Rise and Fall of Ziggy Stardust. Rick Wakeman was the in-house session keyboardist back then, and he can be heard on Bowie albums like "Changes" and "Life On Mars." Trident still remains today and has hosted many renowned artists, including James Taylor and Harry Nilsson. Legendary status was bestowed upon him for hosting The Beatles in July 1968, during the recording of 'Hey Jude,' which ran for more than seven minutes and was the longest song to top the British charts at the time. Trident also cut tracks for the 'White Album' and Abbey Road.

Despite the fact that several tracks were recorded in St Anne's Court, no release date was specified. A contract with the Rondo entertainment agency kept them busy all summer. That August, Mercury Records issued the single 'Earth/Step on Me' in the United States, where it sank without trace due to a lack of promotion. Because the label did not want to waste a promising band and was aware that Brian and Tim had co-written a plethora of material, a possible album or EP was explored. The band was sent to De Lane Lea Studios in Wembley, not the De Lane Lea branch at 129 Kingsway, as claimed elsewhere. Smile collaborated with late producer Fritz Fryer on two original songs and one cover at De Lane Lea, which was created in 1947 and was notable for its work on records by The Beatles, The Stones, The Who, Pink Floyd, ELO, and The Jimi Hendrix Experience during the Sixties. However, the EP was never issued, and the recordings were relegated to the vaults. They would not reappear for another fifteen years, by which time Queen had become superstars. The EP was eventually issued in Japan, where aficionados of oddities can never get enough.

By the end of the year, the band was depressed and on the verge of disbanding. Indeed, Tim Staffell did so: tired with the hardship and poverty of life on the road, he departed, citing Smile as the wrong group for him.

'I was getting a fairly jaundiced view of the music we were making,' he subsequently admitted. 'Then I heard James Brown and said to myself, "God!" ...Essentially, I had switched musical tracks entirely.'

Tim joined Colin Petersen, a former Bee Gees drummer, in the HumpyBong lineup. After one single and one TV appearance, the band was done. Tim eventually opted for a career in special effects, gaining brief fame as the designer of the model trains for television's Thomas the Tank Engine.

Smile's label felt that without its lead singer, they were no longer a band. Roger and Brian's contracts were terminated. Despite their disappointment, they refused to give up. Smile encountered former Blackburn club DJ Terry Yeardon through a friend who may have been Christine Mullen, Brian May's first wife-to-be, and arranged for another recording session. Yeardon was now a maintenance engineer at Pye Studios in London's Marble Arch, notable for having nurtured Petula Clark and for the work of husband-and-wife composing combination Tony Hatch and Jackie Trent, particularly for television themes (Crossroads, Neighbours). Pye also produced Jimi Hendrix's 'Hey Joe' and the Troggs' 'Wild Thing' in 1966, and had previously worked with The Kinks, Richard Harris, and Trini Lopez. Before joining up with Robert Plant and John Bonham to become Led Zeppelin, the studios had even featured Jimmy Page and John Paul Jones as session musicians.

Yeardon, a would-be producer, booked a late-night studio session at Pye for Smile. Acetates of the songs 'Polar Bear' and 'Step on Me' were cut, providing Smile with professional audition material that they could take to other labels. Not that Yeardon expected to see even a smile from Smile again.

Brian, Roger, Tim, and a couple of musicians from the northern band Ibex were now living in a one-bedroom flat in a semi-detached house called 'Carmel' on Ferry Road in Barnes. Helen and Pat McConnell, two sisters who had seen Smile perform in their local pub, had also joined the gang. That small, damp flat would be recalled as 'bohemian' in retrospect. In reality, the flatmates had lived in appalling squalor, with the majority of them sleeping on filthy mattresses on the floor. To make matters worse, they had recently added a new roommate: Freddie Bulsara. What did he recommend they do?

# 6. FRONT MAN

Still infatuated with Jimi Hendrix and inspired by Brian's guitar playing, Freddie acquired a second-hand guitar that he had Tim re-fret and alter to his specifications. Then he went out and got some Teach Yourself books and began learning to play. Freddie had to have realised he'd never be an axe hero. This was not, however, his goal. Suddenly inspired to write and compose original songs, he only needed to know enough guitar chords to get started. Those first composing attempts were like everyone else's: raw, sloppy, and intensely personal. He would quickly learn to take a more abstract approach, delving beneath the surface of his emotions and looking beyond his own experiences, playing with universal themes.

The Ibex boys from Ferry Road were soon joined by the rest of the Liverpool gang who had gathered in London to pursue a record deal. Ken Testi was the road manager for guitarist Mike Bersin, bassist John 'Tupp' Taylor, and drummer Mick 'Miffer' Smith. Ibex were periodically joined by Geoff Higgins, who would play bass so Tupp could play the flute. Ibex performed cover versions of Rod Stewart, The Beatles, and Yes tunes, and frequently began their set with 'Jailhouse Rock,' a mega-hit for Elvis Presley twelve years previously. Even though they were impressive, Freddie couldn't help but observe that they lacked a good vocalist. He'd started showing up at their rehearsals and shows, just like he did with Smile, and would occasionally jump up and sing with Mike Bersin.

'He performed the same kind of performance he did at the pinnacle of his career,' Ken Testi recalled. 'If you know what I mean, he was a star before he was a star. He'd parade about the stage like a puffed-up peacock.'

The band was still in Liverpool, where Freddie was a short-term lodger with Geoff Higgins' family. The Higginses lived above Dovedale Towers on Penny Lane, a street made famous by The Beatles. Freddie slept on the floor in Geoff's room, but he never complained since he was determined to honour his own parents by being the perfect house guest. Ruth, Geoff's mother, is known to have adored him.

Geoff told Mark Hodkinson, author of Queen: The Early Years, that his mother liked him because he spoke properly and was from the South. 'Freddie was really nice to her.'

Despite the fact that the band played as much as they could in the UK in 1969, no record deal was forthcoming. They eventually decided to call it quits. Miffer has family issues and needs a steady income. Richard Thompson, a bandmate, took over as drummer. The new lineup only performed one dismal show. Everything that could go wrong did, including the lights, sound, and equipment. Even the microphone fell short of the mark. Whenever Freddie took the stage as the main man, he twirled his microphone like a majorette's baton. This one came with a bulky and heavy stand. At one point, he grabbed the microphone and attempted to swing it, but the bottom section broke off. Freddie continued with the top half, unfazed. A trademark was created.

The bizarre inconsistencies between Freddie the performer and Fred Bulsara the person became too much to bear. Even on a temporary stage and without ever being named official lead singer, Freddie exuded confidence with every extravagant and histrionic gesture and movement. Offstage, he'd hide in kitchens and cupboards, the makeshift dressing rooms of the pub and club circuit, where he'd struggle coyly into homemade skin-tight clothes so revealing that he couldn't breathe, let alone sit down. Freddie was short, thin, and not conventionally attractive, but he knew he stuck out because of his dark skin and swarthy appearance. His features bothered him at times. When he felt the need to smile, he would hide his dark eyes behind a floppy fringe and his buck teeth behind his palm. When he tried to talk to fans after a show, his natural timidity got the best of him. He was often at a loss for words. Worse, despite his superb English enunciation, his speaking voice was whispery and uncertain. He also lisped a little, which was presumably due to all those teeth. He was the most self-conscious of them all. Only when he was relaxed with friends did his humour and 'real-life' personality shine through, and he allowed himself to openly laugh. When he wasn't on stage, he tried his hardest to blend into the backdrop. Freddie was not yet in the habit of getting drunk or high on drugs - he couldn't afford it, so would make do with the occasional 'girlie' port and lemon in pubs - and he never perfected the knack of projecting confidence among strangers. He was a fish out of water at everyone else's events, no matter how happy and at ease he was on his own.

Freddie became tired of travelling up and down to Liverpool, of never making ends meet, of sleeping on other people's floors in whichever town the band happened to be in. He left Ibex shortly after his twenty-third birthday, moved back to London with Mike Bersin, and began browsing the classifieds.

'I think Ibex filled a gap for Freddie,' Ken Testi would later say. He wanted to sing in a band, and Ibex profited much from his presence. It was a marriage of convenience for everyone involved. We were all quite naive. ..It was Freddie's first used car, the kind of thing you buy when you can scrape together a few dollars. You eventually want a better one.'

Nobody held Freddie responsible for the band's dissolution. Regardless, they all adored him, moved by his ambition, abandon, and exciting desire for life. 'It was an education knowing Freddie,' Ken Testi said, speaking for everyone. He was really dedicated to everything. He had determination, single-mindedness, and a thirst for greatness.'

Bersin and Taylor made their way back to Liverpool. Thompson vanished from the London music scene. The rest of them stayed in their overcrowded West London flat. Freddie was left without a band, and Roger and Brian were left without a lead singer. Why didn't they just buy him?

'Freddie was regarded as a bit of a joke by the Smile folks,' his buddy Chris Dummett subsequently revealed. 'They used to send him up and make fun of him. ..I suppose in an affectionate way.'

Often, the solution right in front of us is the one we miss.

Freddie had begun to struggle with his sexual orientation, as if he didn't have enough to worry about. Despite the fact that he'd already had companions, including a young woman on his course named Rosemary Pearson, several recall him expressing a strong desire to meet gay guys but never having the courage to do so.

'He thought he liked women, but it took him a long time to realise he was gay,' says one former art college associate. ..I don't think he could face the feelings it instilled in him. He was definitely fascinated by homosexuality, but he was also terrified of it. I imagine he was apprehensive about accepting himself as gay.'

Another buddy recalls Freddie paying frequent visits to a group of gay flatmates in Barnes. He kept these visits hidden from his flatmates, unable to explain to them what he couldn't understand himself. Freddie would retreat into his shell and become fairly reclusive from time to time, worrying constantly about the impression he was making. Around the same period, he began to exhibit less appealing characteristics. He could be self-centred and egocentric, not to mention sullen and sulky, as if an internal fight was overwhelming him.

Everyone has a dark side. Freddie was a genuinely good, generous, and considerate person. Instead of exploiting others to gain what he wanted, he seemed content to let himself be used, expecting nothing in return. His vanity was possibly his weakest trait. He would fidget with his hair and clothes incessantly, obsessing over his look. His repeated pronouncements that he will become a "legend" could grate on people's nerves.

His fixation with looks didn't help: while most of his companions were living hand to mouth, Freddie refused to use public transportation, preferring to spend the last cents in his pocket on taxis home when he should have been eating himself. Friends began to lose faith in him. What would happen to Freddie if he didn't make it in the music business, they wondered? Despite his graphic design degree, they knew he'd never work a regular job.

He was insecure because he lacked consistency and direction in every element of his life. Freddie was well aware that he was not like most people. He was also aware that he needed to pay his bills. While he still had his own bedroom at his parents' Feltham home, to which he could return whenever he pleased, he was hesitant to declare defeat and slink home. He knew his family would struggle to grasp his new existence, so he never brought friends home to see his parents or sister.

'As a parent, you worry, but you have to let your child live their life,' Jer, his mother, said.

Freddie continued to return home for dinner once or twice a week, and his mother would always prepare his favourite dish, Dhansak: a delectable if tedious Indian dish famous in the Parsee community that combines elements of Persian and Gujarati cuisine. The dish includes vegetables and lentils, garlic, ginger, and spices, as well as meat (typically mutton) and pumpkin or gourd. Given his poverty at the time, it appears likely that this was the only square meal Freddie ate all week.

During the first cold weeks of 1970, he trudged around London agencies with his art portfolio. Austin Knight in Holborn's Chancery Lane agreed to represent him and pitch for design work on his behalf. Freddie, on the other hand, had had enough of sitting around waiting for the phone to ring. He went freelancing and began putting advertisements. But he spent so much time with Smile at rehearsals and shows that his attention was diverted, and his heart was not in finding himself steady work. There was only one solution: he would have to form his own band. Freddie rebuilt Ibex as Wreckage, with Ibex's former drummer Richard Thompson, Mike Bersin, and Tupp Taylor. Their first live performance was at Ealing College of Art, which was attended by a confused Brian May, Roger Taylor, his flatmates, and a boisterous Kensington contingent. Brian and Roger, who hadn't realised that campy, opinionated Freddie really did 'have something' as a front man, were taken aback. Even if the band's music was unimpressive, Freddie was a crowd pleaser. The gig was a success, and Wreckage were booked to play Imperial College, with a string of rugby club dates to follow.

Freddie remained dissatisfied. He knew he had what it required, but he had a feeling something wasn't quite right. He couldn't tell if he had expected an instant three-album deal with a major record company, or if he simply felt out of sync with Wreckage's overall musical style and ambition. He left the band soon after, vowed to wait for Brian and Roger's pennies to drop, and auditioned for a band named Sour Milk Sea.

George Harrison wrote "Sour Milk Sea" during the sessions for The Beatles' so-called "White Album." It was one of the rare non-Beatles songs to contain at least three of them, recorded by Apple artist Jackie Lomax and released as a single in 1968. It so impressed Chris Dummet (later changed his surname to Chesney) and Jeremy Gallop, two public school friends from St Edward's, Oxford, that they changed the name of their common-room band Tomato City to that of the song. Sour Milk Sea's lineup also included drummer Robert

Tyrrell, who had previously performed in pre-Genesis band The Anon with Mike Rutherford and Anthony Phillips at Charterhouse School. Sour Milk Sea made their début at Guildford City Hall, opening for burgeoning acts Deep Purple, Taste, Blodwyn Pig, and Junior's Eyes - whose enduring claim to fame was serving as David Bowie's backup band in 1969. Mick Wayne, a founding member of Junior's Eyes, would join Rick Wakeman as a guest musician on David Bowie's breakthrough, 'Space Oddity.' Sour Milk Sea went professional in June 1969, well knowing that they needed that certain something. It came in the person of Freddie Bulsara, who showed up at a Dorking church crypt to audition for the role of lead singer and front man. He exuded nonchalance and flair, with his flowing black hair and dandy velvet gear. He was several years older than the boys from the Sour Milk Sea, and it showed. 'Fred Bull' was his name.

'He had an enormous amount of charisma, which is why we chose him,' Jeremy 'Rubber' Gallop, who later became a guitar teacher before dying of pancreatic illness in January 2006, recalled, 'but we were truly spoiled for choice that day. Normally at auditions you'd get four or five guys who were rubbish, but we had two other strong contenders. One was a black man with God's voice but not Fred's looks, while the other was folk singer Bridget St John, dubbed "the female John Martyn" later on.

Freddie joined the band, and was in business. Sour Milk Sea quickly landed a high-profile gig in the ballroom of Oxford's Randolph Hotel, which was packed with debutantes in posh gowns.

'Our sound wasn't great,' Gallop admitted.

'Freddie definitely got what people were there in the palm of his hand, just by sheer aggression and his good looks. He was very posey and camp and quite vain. I remember him coming into my house once and poking his long hair about in the mirror. "I look good today, don't you think, Rubber?" he said. "I was only eighteen at the time, and I didn't find it amusing."

The only other significant Sour Milk Sea performance with Freddie as the front man took place in March 1970 at Highfield Parish Hall in Headington, Oxford, as a benefit for the homeless charity Shelter.

The band gave an interview with the Oxford Mail, which also published the words to Freddie's song, 'Lover', with the classic opening line 'You never had it so good/the yoghurt-pushers are here'. However, after a promising start, old school mates Chesney and Gallop fell out.

'Freddie wants to alter us extremely quickly,' Gallop stated.

'On stage, he took on a different persona. He was just as electrifying as he was later in life. Otherwise he was quite calm. I'll always remember him being strangely quiet and well-mannered. My mum liked him. Rather shamefully, I ended the band.'

Jeremy Gallop was Jonathan Morrish's half-uncle. Former CBS Records and Sony executive Jonathan, who became Michael Jackson's publicist and confidant for twenty-eight years, remembers attending that Oxford gig as a teenager.

'At that stage, Freddie, to me, was Martin Peters,' Jonathan tells me, referring to the 1966 England World Cup soccer legend described by manager Sir Alf Ramsey as being 'ten years ahead of his time'. Peters was blessed with such versatility that he was deployable in every position at West Ham United, including goalkeeper.

'Freddie was this flamboyant showman at a time when bands went on stage dressed in whatever they'd been wearing all day,' says Jonathan.

'That Freddie understood showmanship was plain for all to see, even then. It's hard now for people who weren't there to understand what developing rock music was like. You were in it to be a musician. You were "musician-ly". You lived life. What Freddie knew, intuitively, was the golden rule of showbiz: you make a show. It was what Epstein did with The Beatles. "Mach Schau!", the German promoters used to yell at the boys in Hamburg's Star Club. In other words, it was not just about singing. It was also about the lapel-free jackets, the hairstyles, the bashful grins. The Beatles then spent the next eight years rebelling against all that, as if trying to prove that music was the only thing that mattered. Freddie, even as an embryonic performer, knew otherwise.'

Jonathan knew Michael Jackson intimately until the end of his life. The reasons behind the eventual bond between Freddie and Michael, he says, were obvious to those who knew them both.

'Neither one was simply a musician or a singer. What Freddie did with "Bohemian Rhapsody", Michael recreated with "Thriller". The point being that the great artists just get it. They know instinctively how to be multimedia. Freddie's genius was understanding, not just the song he had written the words and melody to, and how it all sounded, but how you deliver it in a contemporary fashion which the audience will comprehend and absorb. How you record it, how you present it on stage, how you style the video, how you dress. You can just picture him on the shoot: "Guys! Make-up, frocks, action!" Who the fuck wore make-up? Men didn't. In 1970, if you wore moisturiser you were dismissed as "queer" – the word of the day. Yet all these years later, the men's cosmetics industry is worth billions. As I said, he was way ahead of his time. Even in 1970, Freddie was saying "NO, guys, this is what showbiz is about!"'

For as long as Queen have existed, an error has prevailed regarding alternative names that the band considered calling themselves.

'Brian and Roger had both read the same trilogy of books by C.S. Lewis during their childhood – Out of the Silent Planet – from which the phrase the Grand Dance had come', explained Jacky Gunn and Jim Jenkins in Queen's 'official biography' As It Began (1992). This information has been repeated in so many Queen and Freddie Mercury books that it has become 'fact' – even appearing as such on Queen's official website, where Queen expert Rhys Thomas, in 'A Review' (7 March 2011) discusses The Grand Dance, The Rich Kids (later picked up by Sex Pistol Glen Matlock as the name of his new group), and Build Your Own Boat as other names that Queen had discussed. In an interview with Q magazine, March 2011, Brian said, 'We had a list of suggested names, and Queen had come from Freddie. One of the others was the Grand Dance, which I don't think would have been very good . ..'

In fact, the reference is erroneous. Out of the Silent Planet is the first novel of the Lewis sci-fi trilogy referred to as 'the Space Trilogy', 'the Cosmic Trilogy' or 'the Ransom Trilogy'. The other two volumes in the collection, which was itself inspired by David Lindsay's A Voyage to Arcturus (1920), are Perelandra and That Hideous Strength. In the second novel, Perelandra, Lewis introduces a new Garden of Eden on the planet Venus, an alternative Adam and Eve, and a new serpent figure to tempt them. The author explores what might have come to pass had Eve resisted temptation and avoided the Fall of Man. It is in Perelandra that we find our Queen reference: a description of the mystical experience of seeing directly into 'the GREAT Dance' – not 'Grand' – of the multi-dimensional space-time-consciousness continuum that is the time cosmos: 'So with the Great Dance. Set your eyes on one movement and it will lead you through all patterns and it will seem to you the master movement. But the seeming will be there . ..there seems no plan because it is all plan: there seems no centre because it is all centre. Blessed be He!'

One-word titles work better, Freddie argued. They are infinitely more memorable. They have more punch. Freddie's own outrageous suggestion was 'Queen'. The others resisted with snorts and scorn, primarily because of the word's homosexual connotations. 'Gay' was a word rarely heard at that time. It probably emerged eventually in defiance of 'queer', its disparaging predecessor. Although Freddie had not 'come out' – nor would he ever officially do so – he was used to being called 'an old queen'. He rather liked it. He swooned at its androgyny and adored its regal whiff. Even better, the name would give him the perfect excuse to camp it to the hilt on stage. Brian and Roger soon came round, having seen the funny side. The point being that no male could be more macho, more straight nor more besotted by women than those two. In their terms, to be called 'Queen' was ironic, and it worked.

Having agreed to the band's identity, Freddie set about renaming himself. Bulsara was dropped in favour of Mercury, the ancient Roman messenger of the gods. Like Hermes, his Greek counterpart, Mercury was represented with winged sandals and a staff entwined with snakes. Also the name of the common liquid metal long ago familiar in Chinese and Hindu culture and found in ancient Egyptian tombs, 'Mercury' identifies the planet closest to the Sun as well, which has no moons.

Many theories have arisen over the years as to why Freddie chose that surname. According to Queen fan and author Jim Jenkins, 'Freddie told me himself in 1975, that it was after the messenger of the gods. I remember it as if he's just said it to me. People have said since that it was after Mike Mercury in TV's Fireball XL5, but I can tell you for sure that it was nothing to do with him.'

According to Brian May's memory: 'Freddie had written this song called "My Fairy King", and there's a line in it that says, "Oh Mother Mercury what have you done to me?" [The lyric actually reads: Mother mercury mercury/look what they've done to me/I cannot run, I cannot hide.]

'And it was after that that he said, "I am going to become Mercury as the mother in this song is my mother." And we were like, "Are you mad?"

'Changing his name was part of him assuming this different skin,' adds May. 'The young Bulsara was still there, but for the public he was going to be this god.'

Although it has been widely assumed that Freddie changed his name by deed poll in or around 1970, nothing exists to prove this. While they were able to supply Elton John's, there is no official entry for Freddie at the Public Records Office, now the National Archives, in Kew, West London. As an official there told me, 'Only ten per cent of name changes are registered through the Supreme Court and therefore appear on our records. These days, in fact, it's about five per cent. It is not a legal requirement: you can call yourself whatever you like. Chances are that Mr Mercury changed his name through his solicitor. When the documentation is drawn up, he'd keep half and the solicitor would keep half.'

Freddie later revealed his fascination with mythology and astrology, by designing Queen's now legendary logo. Its principal figure is a spread-winged phoenix, the symbol of immortality remembered fondly by Freddie from the crest of his alma mater, St Peter's in

Panchgani. The logo also incorporated the zodiac signs of each band member: two lions, for the Leos, Taylor and Deacon, a crab for Cancerian May, and a couple of fairies for Virgoan Mercury, complete with a stylised 'Q' and elaborate crown.

Other commitments notwithstanding, the band were ready to play their debut gig as Queen: a Red Cross benefit at City Hall, Truro in Cornwall, Britain's most south westerly point. The show, which took place on 27 June 1970, was co-arranged by Roger's mother Win Hitchens, and the line-up featured Mike Grose on bass (he lasted only three shows). Their opening number was 'Stone Cold Crazy', based on an energetic Wreckage number. But it fell a bit flat in that half-empty venue. Observers remembered that the band were not yet 'tight' enough, nor Freddie coordinated enough.

'Freddie was not like how he became,' commented Roger's mum Win. 'He had not got his movements off properly.'

But: 'Freddie had real ambitions for the band,' remembers his sister Kashmira. 'He had this complete determination to succeed.'

A show at Imperial College on 18 July followed, their set made up almost exclusively of cover versions – everything from James Brown and Little Richard to Buddy Holly and Shirley Bassey – and just two original compositions: 'Stone Cold Crazy', which featured the whole group as co-writers, and 'Liar'.

'We did more heavy rock 'n' roll with the Queen delivery to give people something they could get hold of – get on, sock it to 'em, get off,' commented Brian.

Mike Grose was replaced by bass player Barry Mitchell, who performed with Queen at eleven shows from summer until Christmas, in London colleges, Liverpool's famous Cavern Club and a couple of church halls. The Queen still hadn't found the one they were looking for.

Now that Roger had enrolled at North London Polytechnic to study Biology, he would get a grant to supplement his meagre income. This left Freddie the only Queen member not engaged in tertiary education. Not that it bothered any of them. Queen threw themselves at the live circuit with renewed vigour. That September, Brian arranged a showcase at Imperial College and invited a number of top London booking agents. Although several turned up, none were impressed enough to offer Queen a tour. Hungry for fame and success, they took this badly.

Tragedy struck in Freddie's life (and many shared the sadness) on 18 September 1970, when his idol Jimi Hendrix died. The definitive rock musician who had famously performed the Star-Spangled Banner at the Woodstock Festival the previous year, who had just opened his own state-of-the-art recording studio, Electric Lady, in Greenwich Village, New York, and who had only the previous month played for his biggest-ever audience – 600,000 people at the Isle of Wight Festival – was found dead in a pool of red wine vomit at girlfriend Monika Dannemann's Samarkand Hotel apartment in Notting Hill. While insiders would claim for years that Hendrix was murdered, the most likely cause of his death was an overdose of the sedative Vesparax, ingested with excess alcohol. Dannemann later committed suicide.

Freddie was inconsolable. Too devastated to work, he and Roger closed their stall as a mark of respect. Later that day, while rehearsing at Imperial College, virtually on the doorstep of the scene of Hendrix's death, Brian, Roger and Freddie played their own personal tribute in a jam session of 'Voodoo Chile', 'Purple Haze', 'Foxy Lady' and other now immortal Hendrix hits.

The perfect bass player continued to elude the trio. Not until February 1971 did they run into John Deacon by chance at a London disco. Leicester-born Deacon, who had been involved with bands since the age of fourteen, was an Electronics undergraduate at Chelsea College. A man of few words, he made up for it with an acute sense of rhythm and a restless brain. He was also a dab hand with amplifiers and other music equipment, and was looking for a band to join.

More than that, says Roger: 'We thought he was great. We were all so used to each other, and we're so over the top, we thought that because he was quiet he would fit in with us without too much upheaval. He was a great bass player too – and the fact that he was a wizard with electronics was definitely a deciding factor.'

From February 1971 until Queen's final gig on 9 August 1986, the band line-up remained exactly the same.

Six months of intense rehearsal ensued as Brian, John and Freddie set about teaching John their repertoire. At the time, John was still a student, while Brian was working on his thesis. They still regarded Queen as an extracurricular hobby. Only Roger and Freddie could devote their time totally to Queen, and had set their hearts on a full-blown rock 'n' roll career. On 11 July 1971, Queen began an eleven-date tour of Cornwall, culminating in the outdoor Tregye Festival of Contemporary Music on 21 August. Further gigs followed throughout the Michaelmas term, including another at Imperial College on 6 October, an appearance at Epsom Swimming Baths on 9 December, and a New Year's Eve show at Twickenham's London Rugby Club.

Roger, meanwhile, had lost interest in the market stall. The novelty has worn off, but worse, it has started to feel 'undignified'. He quit the 'Kasbah', leaving Freddie to team up with fellow stallholder Alan Mair. Freddie remained as enthusiastic as ever about the Kensington scene. Not just because he was a deep-dyed mover and shaker. He had fallen in love.

# 7. MARY

Mary Austin embodied a Hulanicki Biba poster, with her apricot hair, green eyes, and Bambi lashes. Barbara Hulanicki, the fashion designer who built the Kensington emporium that spawned a thriving fashion trend, may have selected Mary as her muse. Mary, little and fine-boned, made up for her lack of stature and confidence with nearly textbook Seventies style.

Mick Rock, a London-born Cambridge Modern Languages graduate and alumnus of the London Film School, went into professional photography after the late Syd Barrett (former lead vocalist of Pink

Floyd) asked Rock to photograph him for the cover of his solo album The Madcap Laughs. Rock, his true name, became involved in Seventies drug culture and befriended David Bowie, becoming his official photographer. He is credited not only with chronicling the music scene - 'The Man Who Shot the Seventies' - but also with helping to create it. He shot some of the initial publicity photos for Freddie and Queen before going on to create famous album artwork for Queen II and Sheer Heart Attack. Rock has lived in New York since 1977, after being absorbed in the underground scene produced by The Ramones, Talking Heads, and David Bowie.

'Freddie was already living with Mary when I met him, so I got to know and love them both equally,' Rock explains. 'I was always coming round to their tiny flat to hang out with them at teatime. Freddie loved tea. Mary was a wonderfully cute-looking lady who could have had anyone and done anything at the height of the Glam Rock craze. But she never considered herself as anything remarkable. She never wanted to put herself forward in any way. She was humble, lovely, and charming. You just wanted to cuddle with her.'

She had the demeanour of an earlier namesake, Mary Hopkin - the fresh-faced prodigy of Paul McCartney who'd had a hit with 'Those Were the Days'. The Marys shared a chaste, untouchable, ethereal aspect that complimented the day's bohemian clothing. What would later be dubbed 'the Stevie Nicks style' after the Fleetwood Mac singer was already popular on Kensington High Street: midi skirts, maxi jackets, suede platform boots, chiffon scarves, velvet chain chokers, purple lips, and smokey eyelids.

'She'd had a difficult upbringing,' recalls dependable journalist David Wigg. 'Her parents were deaf and dumb, and they communicated through sign language and lip-reading. Her father worked as a hand-trimmer for wallpaper specialists, while her mother was a domestic for a small business. But that wouldn't have troubled Freddie. He wasn't interested in toffs. He seemed to appreciate folks who were a little below his own level. I always believed it was an insecurity thing. He was drawn to those who were artistic or who had overcome adversity. He was artistic and humorous, and he loved to laugh. Mary was bashful, yet she could make him laugh.'

A nineteen-year-old trainee secretary when she won her work at Biba, she has been described variously as having been a 'PR', 'secretary', 'sales girl', 'floor manager' and 'manager'. Whatever her function, or roles, at the famous fashion emporium, shopping seems a strange career choice for a shy young woman who found talking difficult growing up in a largely silent environment. The incense-filled, fern-adorned boutique was a noisy, crowded Aladdin's Cave, loaded with clothes, shoes, make-up, jewellery, bags, and stunning sales girls. The many music and movie stars who came to the club mixed freely with the fashion-conscious, many of whom were 'just seeking' for a Jagger or a McCartney.

Despite her modest demeanour, Mary found herself immersed in London's rock scene. Brian May was the first to notice her at an Imperial College gig one night in 1970, and the two struck up a conversation.

She was just his type of gal in many respects. Brian, the tall, dark, and dishy one, lost no time in asking Mary out. They got along, but their interactions were dull. Brian quickly realised that things were not going to progress past friendship. Freddie, on the other hand, had a different opinion. Freddie got the girl of his dreams after pestering Brian for an introduction.

The affinity between them was immediate, mutual, and would endure a lifetime. It's puzzling, therefore, that Mary spent the following six months attempting to avoid him, even dating other men - but none seriously. Years later, she explained that she did so because she thought Freddie was more interested in her buddy than in her. After one of the band's shows, she left him at the bar with her girlfriend, excused herself to go to the Ladies, and vanished into the night. Freddie was taken aback, but he was unfazed. Mary pretended to be busy that night when he invited her out on a date for his twenty-fourth birthday, September 5, 1970.

'I was trying to look cool,' she explained to David Wigg. 'Not because I couldn't go. Freddie, on the other hand, was not deterred. We went out the next day instead. He wanted to see Mott the Hoople at the Marquee Club in Soho. We didn't have much money back then, so we just did basic things like any other young people. There were no lavish dinners; they came later, when he made it big.'

The couple became inseparable and began a sexual relationship almost immediately. Their relationship would take precedence over any affair, man or woman, in which Freddie would eventually engage.

Freddie and Mary have a lot in common. Each had felt distanced from their parents and had succumbed to the impulse to assert their individuality. Each had a 'tip of the iceberg' personality that revealed little of their true selves. Each may give the impression of being shallow, flippant, and frivolous, with materialistic tendencies and a live-for-the-moment attitude, especially when they were younger. But most of it came down to appearance and the careful concealing of underlying timidity. Both were incredibly sensitive, naturally guarded, and deeper than they appeared. The fact that they recognized themselves in each other created the foundation of a fascinating and eternal bond. As they grew older, the more opposing and paradoxical components of their personalities began to blend. Mary may appear to be a lovely soul who wouldn't hurt a fly, but her frail exterior veiled an inner strength and serenity that Freddie admired dearly, maybe because he worried that the 'Great Pretender' in him lacked those attributes. Although Mary was aware that Freddie had family in Feltham, it would be some time before he brought his girlfriend home to meet them. It's easy to see why: Mary was all the Bulsaras could have hoped for in a daughter-in-law. They would almost certainly have put pressure on their son to marry her and provide them with the grandkids they desired. Freddie wasn't ready for anything like marriage. Little did his family know at the time that he would never be.

Mary became Freddie's rock over time. He would rely on her to be strong for him. Whenever Freddie thought his sex/drugs/rock 'n' roll lifestyle was out of control, and he was unable to cope with the stresses of recording and touring, he resorted to Mary. She was the mother figure to whom he would always cling, solid and reliable, ever-forgiving and all-accepting.

'Mary Austin was Freddie's mother in a way,' says music publicist Bernard Doherty.

'She was there for him every moment of every day, putting her own life on hold to do so. She followed him. She never left his side. He was obviously committed to her. She clearly filled the void left by what his parents should have been to him when he was a child. Instead, they threw him on a ship and sent him to school hundreds of miles away, a journey that took roughly sixty days back then. He was eight years old. Can you imagine? In his deepest psyche, he would never have resolved that. Then there was Mary. McCartney sang "Mother Mary Comes to Me" on "Let It Be" in 1970, didn't he?: ironically, the year Mary and Freddie met.

With its matriarchal Blessed Virgin Mary symbolism, it may have become their theme song. Mary was the Mary in that song. She was pure. In the end, not even Freddie was sleeping with her. ..'

Because Freddie had chosen to be gay by this point, making Mary a born-again virgin?

'The myth was preserved,' Bernard says, nodding. 'In his mind, she was ideal, and she was all for him. Mary existed solely for the sake of Freddie.'

'Mary was clearly a mother figure,' says consulting psychiatrist Dr Cosmo Hallstrom.

'More to the point, the idealised mother figure: symbolic of exactly what he thought a woman should be. Freddie was very sexual and didn't care who he had sex with. He could have wonderful sex with her while still rushing off to have a lot of illicit and brutal encounters elsewhere. Those were typically unstable and fleeting partnerships. He always returned to her. And, of course, she was always waiting for him, limiting herself to her guy.

'She looked after him, mothered him, dealt with the nice side of Freddie. She was his foundation and his strength. What he had with her allowed him to go off and have his flirtations. As a result, she became the long-suffering wife as well as the matriarch, putting up with all kinds of crap. But she served an important purpose: the suffering his guilt gave him, and the way he behaved when she wasn't around, was the key to his creativity. A contented individual does not feel the urge to do or create anything. Happy individuals are pleased with their lot in life, with the way things are. Freddie was always in pain. The way he felt about Mary was the cause of this, but it was also a motivation for his work.'

Freddie's sentiments for Mary were termed as 'Mother Love' by some. It's no wonder that this became the title of a sombre piece sung by Freddie and Brian on Queen's Made in Heaven album, released four years after Mercury's death in 1991.

Freddie once defined himself as "a man of extremes." 'I have a soft side and a hard side, with not much in between. If the proper person finds me, I can be incredibly vulnerable, a real baby, which is typically when I get trampled. But when I'm tough, no one can touch me.'

Mary also knew that Freddie had suffered from a persecution complex since infancy, something he rarely admitted to. That is, he was concerned that people were making fun of him behind his back, and that he was actually foolish. It proved to be one of his most ferocious inner demons till his death.

Fear might not have been so unjustified after all. 'To be honest, everyone believed that Freddie was a bit of a wally,' says Peter 'Ratty' Hince, a long-serving Queen roadie who now works as a photographer. Even though it was glam, Freddie was over the top. That flowing costume stuff. I didn't believe he was particularly strong back then. They were all very much a unit.'

Perhaps his anger with this complex was what prompted him to erupt in rage at times. Freddie's temper would flare up inexplicably, causing him to be harsh and even vicious, spewing scathing put-downs and gratuitously caustic comments. While it has been stated that Mary developed a defensive streak to protect Freddie and subsequently herself from the media and hangers-on, and that she could be untrusting and suspicious, could she actually have been protecting them both from Freddie himself?

Their union was a meeting of the heart, intellect, and soul, but the body could not be overlooked. Freddie's sexual relationship with Mary lasted six years. That is a long period in one's early twenties, and it indicates great dedication. They soon began living together, in a small, shabby £10-a-week bedsit in Victoria Road, close off Kensington High Street - the London neighbourhood to which Freddie would always return. Today, the street is officially the most expensive in England and Wales for property, with the average home valued at £6.4 million.

Two years later, the couple would move to a larger, self-contained but ruinously damp apartment on Holland Road, which would cost £9 more per week.

'We grew up together. 'I liked him, and it progressed from there,' Mary would recall. 'It took me about three years to really fall in love. I've never felt that way before or since with anyone. ..I adored Freddie.

'I felt extremely protected with him,' she subsequently told David Wigg.

'The more I got to know him, the more I liked him for himself. He was a person of character, which I believe is becoming unusual in today's world. ..We knew we could rely on each other. ..and that we would never intentionally hurt each other.

'One Christmas, he purchased me a ring and placed it in the largest box. I opened the box, and within was another box, and so on until I arrived at this extremely small box. When I opened it, there was this stunning Egyptian scarab ring inside. It is said to bring good luck. He was really polite and shy about handing it to me.'

'Whatever else was going on,' Mick Rock adds, 'Freddie was living this nice little home life with Mary, and it was all very cosy and charming. When I went around there, Freddie was always in his dressing robe and slippers. We could sit and speak for hours.'

Mary has made a point of refusing to address even the most ordinary parts of their relationship. However, private information has emerged in a few interviews. For example, during their years together, anytime Freddie had a burst of songwriting inspiration in the middle of the night, he would drag his piano close to the bed and continue composing. The normal woman would not have put up with that for long.

If Mary had reservations about Freddie's sexuality, she sought to dismiss them at first.

'I once told her,'surely you must have wondered if Freddie was gay,' David Wigg recalled. "But everywhere we went, girls were going crazy for him," she told me. "When he came off stage, they were all over him." After one specific concert where he was besieged by ladies, she actually started walking away, thinking, "Freddie doesn't need me any longer." He spotted her leaving and raced after her. "Where are you going?""You don't need me," Mary said to him, "you have all this." "I do need you," Freddie replied. "I want you to be part of it." '

'Later, he started coming home very late at night, and I started thinking "this is it,"' she informed David.

'Mary informed me that at first she assumed he was seeing another lady. "I thought he didn't want me any longer," she explained. He'd always have an excuse: 'we've been recording, dear,' or 'we got carried away, sorry I'm so late,' she said. He ultimately came in one evening and said, "Mary, there's something I have to tell you." She was still convinced there was another lady and braced herself. To her relief, he simply stated, "I think I'm bisexual."

'"No, Freddie, I don't think you're bisexual," she told him. "I think you're gay."

'Freddie was mortified in a way,' she told me. But he did accept it from her nearly immediately. When he eventually moved into Garden Lodge in Kensington, he purchased her a modest home around the corner, where she could view his large mansion from the bathroom window.'

She soon became the matriarch of Freddie's 'family,' a predominantly gay retinue of staff who doubled as pals.

'Freddie had an open and honest relationship with Mary that he could never have had with his birth mother due to family religion, culture, and so on,' Wigg says.

Mick Rock recalls Freddie being 'beside himself' with his sexuality difficulties.

'This was before he finally came out of the closet. He was certainly gay, but not entirely gay, and that screwed him over. He was torn. It was almost as if he needed to know if he was one thing or the other, but he was stuck in the middle, in a kind of no man's land. He had a thing for ladies. He had a great time with them. Later in life, it could have been mostly men for sex. ..He was more promiscuous with guys, but he loved to get with the girls. Of course, Mary was his true love. ..He had never known a closer emotional attachment. The greatest irony in Freddie's life was that, despite being fundamentally gay, his most important connection was with a woman. Perhaps it had more to do with the woman in issue than her sexual orientation. Between him and Mary, there was sincere affection. The sexual aspect was secondary to their emotional and spiritual tie.'

Freddie was soon taking male lovers, though he never brought them home to the bedsit he shared with Mary. At first, he acted discreetly, maintaining the façade of his heterosexual domestic relationship. Mary pampered him and turned a blind eye, hoping that it was simply a 'phase'. But, as time passed, it became clear that he preferred his own gender. Finally, he couldn't keep the truth hidden any longer and confessed.

'I could see he was uneasy with something,' Mary told David Wigg. So hearing it was reassuring. I appreciated his candour with me. I don't think he expected my backing, but I couldn't deny Freddie the chance to be at peace with himself.'

It speaks a lot about the woman that she parked her personal anguish over broken dreams and enabled their relationship to evolve into a close, platonic friendship. She became Freddie's Girl Friday and spent at least part of every day with him from then on. She identified herself as his "general dogsbody." Freddie dubbed her 'Old Faithful'.

Mary was now free to look for another companion. It would be a long time before she did so.

She couldn't let go, apparently suggesting to Freddie that they have a kid together, to which he allegedly answered that he would 'rather have a cat'. Mary would go on to have two sons: Richard, Freddie's godson, and Jamie, born shortly after Freddie died. But many of her relationships with men seemed doomed to fail, maybe because Freddie cast long shadows and was always under her skin. Piers Cameron, the boys' father, arrived and departed.

'He had always felt overshadowed by Freddie,' Mary explained.

Freddie, despite the never-ending stream of boyfriends, would have more affairs with women. Mary could only accept this since she had chosen to stay a part of Freddie's life. Most people who knew them both feel that no other lady ever replaced Mary in Freddie's affections. The fact that he gave her his home and the majority of his income undoubtedly supports this.

'Mary is nothing short of a saint,' says Mick Rock. 'She's amazing. Terrific. Extremely devoted. Unpretentious. Unintrusive. A good person. One of the most wonderful people I've ever known. I'd frequently see Freddie in New York after Queen had made it and I'd moved to Manhattan. We'd hang out and talk. Years later, while I was in London, I had tea with Mary, and she said something quite weird to me. I didn't comprehend it at the time, but I believe I do now. "First my father, then Freddie, and now my sons," she explained. "It appears that I was put on this earth to nurture men," she seemed to be saying. When you think about it, it's an odd life. But it makes sense.'

Rock was relieved that Freddie had treated her well.

'He was one-of-a-kind, and anyone would have had difficulty dealing with that. Also, he was more focused on his work than anything else. To make matters worse, he'd have these bizarre outbursts. He must have been a misery to work with and live with. He was well aware of it. He wasn't stupid. What Mary had to put up with was more than most people could bear, but she never stopped loving him. Not to this day. You might say she devoted her life for him, and what she got in return is nothing compared to what she gave, believe me.'

'He extended the tapestry of my life so much by introducing me to the realms of ballet, opera, and art,' Mary would later remark. I've learnt a lot from him, and he's given me a lot. I'd never want to abandon him.'

None of this made him any easier to deal with. Not only did he make a drama out of every situation, but everything had to be exact. Even vases of flowers around the house had to be perfectly arranged or he would throw them outdoors in anger.

'It was all because of his personality,' Mary explained. 'He liked things done his way, and he could be demanding. We fought a lot. But he enjoyed a good row.'

Years later, long after his death, Mary would come to terms with the money Freddie had left her and find happiness again in his magnificent Georgian home. This was with Nick, the London businessman she married privately on Long Island in 1998, with only her sons as witnesses.

'I believe Nick was extremely gutsy to take me on,' she told David Wigg. 'I arrive with a lot of baggage. ..As life progresses. ..I can appreciate what I had and what I currently have and move on with my life.'

'Some people criticised her for the manner she hung in there, and they all questioned her intentions,' adds her friend Mick Rock. But I can tell you she wasn't there for the money. I'd put my life on it.'

People could say whatever they wanted. Those who could count recognized the 'his' and 'hers' of the situation (every story has at least three sides). Mary had kept her own counsel for twenty-one years. Freddie's loyalty spoke for itself. Why didn't she face the truth, leave town, and start a new life? Could her innermost fear have been that she would be nothing without him?

'That she persisted in a circumstance in which most women would have fled to find a heterosexual setting. ..is a marvel of perseverance and, it must be admitted, acting,' remarked Freddie's close friend and confidant David Evans.

'I honestly believe she was never at ease among the gay society with which Freddie surrounded himself,' he stated in his 1995 biography More of the Real Life.

'I could sense she was uncomfortable and, to the best of my ability, compensated for it by purposefully toning down parts of my own behaviour to accommodate her fundamentally heterosexual femininity. Mary was never "one of the boys," as so many ladies in Freddie's life were. She didn't seem to have Barbara Valentin's magnificent, exuberant self-assurance. ..or Anita Dobson or Diana Moseley. ..Freddie's outrageousness did not threaten any of these great, talented, and strong ladies. In fact, it validated them.

'Mary was always detached, removed in spirit and body from The Real Life [as Freddie's family set-up was referred to by insiders].'

While Freddie and his friends were overjoyed when she began dating Piers Cameron and became pregnant with the first of their two kids, no one was surprised when the affair ended. 'That she remained a part of The Real Life is evident,' Evans added. He hoped Mary would free herself from "the unhealthy clinging-on to a situation that could only ever compound the initial grief and heartbreak, from which it is obvious that she had never recovered."


# 8. TRIDENT

1971 was almost finished, and Queen were still nowhere fast, despite performing as many performances as Brian and John's scholastic schedules would allow, and despite everyone's best efforts to get them signed. 'If we were going to drop the careers we'd worked so hard for, we wanted to do a really fantastic job of music,' Brian said. We all had a lot to lose, and it didn't come easily. To be honest, none of us anticipated it would take three years to get somewhere. It was most emphatically not a fairytale.'

'At one time, two or three years after we started, we were on the verge of disbanding,' Freddie explained. We thought it wasn't working, that there were too many sharks in the industry, and that it was all too much for us. But something inside kept us going, and we learned from our mistakes and successes.'

On another occasion, he would contradict his earlier evaluation, saying, 'There was never a doubt, darling, never. I had a feeling we'd make it. I told everyone who inquired about it.'

Roger recalled those times with fondness.

'Nothing actually happened for the first two years,' he acknowledged. 'We were all studying, but there was no development in the band. We had excellent ideas, though, and I think we all thought we'd make it.'

Queen had tasks to complete. They continued to hound every record label in London, confident in their skill as musicians and persuaded they melded well as a group. They also performed live at every opportunity, taking any college gig they could get. Some were well-attended, while others were not. Tony Stratton-Smith, the Charisma label's head, expressed early interest in Queen and made them a hefty offer of £20,000. They might have done worse than sign with the football-crazed Brummie, an eccentric like Freddie. Strat, a hard drinker, racehorse owner, and homosexual former journalist, had nearly averted death in the 1958 Munich plane disaster, which took twenty-three lives, including eight of Manchester United's 'Busby Babes'; he had elected to cover a World Cup qualifier at the last minute. He became a rock manager and label owner in the late 1960s, working out of a little office on Dean Street in Soho. In 1970, he signed with Genesis and supported Monty Python's albums, as well as Peter Gabriel, Lindisfarne, Van der Graaf Generator, Malcolm McClaren, and Julian Lennon. Strat was known as 'the man who made dreams come true' by his artists.

Even though they were destined for each other, the Queen would not be wooed by the late, great Strat. Rumour has it that the Queen felt they would always be second fiddle to Genesis. They leveraged Charisma's offer and enthusiasm to gain interest from other labels, figuring that if they were worth twenty grand to Strat, they must be worth more elsewhere.

'We were conscious of the sharks the moment we created a demo,' Freddie remembered in 1974. "We had so many incredible offers from individuals saying, "We'll make you the next T. Rex," but we were very careful not to go right in. We visited nearly every company before settling on one. We didn't want to be considered just another band.'

'In the sense that we're convinced of what we're doing,' Brian subsequently stated. If someone tells us it's crap, our attitude is that the individual is mistaken, not that we are rubbish.'

'We wanted to be first,' Freddie would explain. 'We were not going to settle for anything less.'

In other words, the Queen did not think they were good. They were aware of it.

What has been portrayed elsewhere as an accidental meeting with John Anthony, one of London's brightest young record producers at the time, was most likely less of a pleasant coincidence and more of a classic Freddie planned confrontation. Freddie, who was well-known in Kensington and Chelsea for his eclectic musical and sartorial influences, continued to dress up in exotic attire and cruise 'Ken High' and the King's Road on Saturday afternoons, usually after sweet-talking a friend into guarding his market stall. He'd swan around in his element, telling everyone about his idols - at the time, Liza Minnelli, The Who, Led Zeppelin, and David Bowie's Ziggy. With the remark 'you never know who you could meet,' he rationalised the absurd amounts of time he spent on his increasingly odd appearance. Freddie wanted to be noticed, and by someone specific.

His diligence in perambulation paid off. Eventually, John Anthony and Freddie came face to face during a usual Saturday swagger.

Freddie had charmed an invitation to bring the band to Anthony's flat to discuss their career in no time.

Given Anthony's notoriety, this was quite the coup. Anthony began producing after recording for Yes in 1968. He was a former London club DJ at venues such as The Speakeasy, The Roundhouse, and UFO. He had previously worked with Genesis, Van der Graaf Generator, and Lindisfarne as a Strat's associate. 'There's one perfect way to do an album, and four hundred wrong ways,' he once said.

Following the encounter, Anthony persuaded Barry Sheffield, co-owner of Trident Studios with his brother Norman, to join him at a Queen concert at Southeast London's now-defunct 'Forest Hill Hospital' on Friday, March 24, 1972. Until that point, the Sheffields had only heard Queen's five-song tape but had never seen them live. Before committing his company to a deal, Barry wanted to see what they were like live. Sheffield was so taken with Queen's performance that he wanted to sign them right away, especially after their camp interpretation of Shirley Bassey's legendary 'Hey Big Spender'.

'Trident was the best studio in the world,' John Anthony explained, 'which is why it was booked twenty-four hours a day.'

The Sheffield brothers had recently launched Trident Audio Productions, a subsidiary of their company, with a groundbreaking master plan to sign acts, place them in Trident's own state-of-the-art studios, and then negotiate pressing and distribution deals with mainstream record labels for the actual recordings. Although the Queen was aware that beggars could not be choosers, this was not what she was looking for. The Sheffields were a pair of astute businessmen who had shivered many a log in their time. They sat bouncing ballparks at the band until their eyes glazed over, acutely business-minded. What Queen missed in the fine print was that the proposed agreement was a package incorporating two other unrelated acts: Irish singer-songwriter Eugene Wallace and a group called Headstone. The Sheffields' references to managerial control were equally concerning. What they were providing was a one-stop management and recording arrangement in which Trident would manage, produce, record, and song-publish Queen while also negotiating a record company deal on their behalf. All the Queen saw were potential conflicts of interest. Despite their emphasis on subcontracting every component of the agreement, Queen was uneasy at the prospect of Trident managing every area of their career.

They dithered for about eight months before signing the contract, until November 1972, during which time they did not perform a single live event.

'I told them to keep quiet,' John Anthony explained. 'I wanted them to focus on getting their sound together so they could come back and play bigger gigs,' says the producer.

Given that no one of consequence remembers, the reasons for their protracted postponement remain unknown. With no lengthy legal wranglings, perhaps the band was up to their old antics again, using the Trident offer to lure better ones. If they were hoping for a better bargain from the Sheffields, they were let down. The deal Queen eventually signed was a shambles. They would not realise how bad it was for quite some time.

To be fair, Trident and the Sheffields had a good reputation. They not only ran one of London's finest studios, which was frequently used by A-list artists, but they were also not known for unethical business practices. They expected and were entitled to a return on their investment of time and money in Queen. Only Brian would appreciate their role in the Queen's success later in life. The rest of the band didn't care by that point.

'As far as Queen are concerned, our old management is deceased,' Freddie would explain after the final termination of their partnership with Trident. They no longer exist in any manner with us. ..We are overjoyed!'

The arrangement seemed too good to be true to the outside world: the top recording studios in the world granted an unbroken band use of the studios and all facilities. Queen could record their entire debut album with producers John Anthony and his friend Roy Thomas Baker, who would then do the legwork and promote it to companies. Not as nice as it appeared: the band, already embarrassed by the fact that no record company was interested, would now have access to a recording studio only during 'down-time,' when it was not required by paying clients such as David Bowie or Elton John.

'They'd ring and say David Bowie had finished a few hours early, so we'd have from three a.m. until 7:00 a.m. when the cleaners arrived,' Brian confessed. 'A lot of stuff was done in that manner. There were a few complete days, but mostly snippets.'

The setup was not conducive to innovation. It's ironic, then, that a significant recording from the Trident era that is now a very collectible object was created by accident. Queen were waiting in the studio one day when producer Robin Cable invited them to record cover versions of the Phil Spector/Ellie Greenwich composition, 'I Can Hear Music,' with which The Beach Boys had a Top Ten hit in 1969, and 'Goin' Back,' written by husband-and-wife songwriting team Gerry Goffin and Carole King and first recorded by The Byrds. Freddie sang as Brian and Roger played and harmonised. Each Queen member was paid a little amount. None of them could have predicted how renowned, and eventually lucrative, those recordings would become. Queen had signed nothing and agreed to nothing, but they had ceded their claim to control over the finished product by default and in ignorance. The recording was released the next year by EMI under the fictitious moniker Larry Lurex, in both homage and parody of Gary Glitter. However, the gag backfired. The dig outraged most high-profile British DJs, who were strongly protective of The Leader at the time (much before Glitter's famously awful fall from grace). The record sold few copies and was sent to the bargain bins due to insignificant airplay. Years later, it would be re-released and become the highly sought-after disc it is today, changing hands for varying fortunes. Queen, having learned the methods of the cutthroat record industry, eventually acquired the rights to the record themselves.

Queen bit the bullet and began the haphazard process of making their first album that summer. But not with John Anthony. With day-job responsibilities to recording with Al Stewart and an inability to tolerate constant strain, Anthony fell in the studio one night. After his doctor diagnosed him with EBV, a debilitating virus that causes chronic exhaustion, Anthony went on an extended vacation to

Greece, leaving Queen in the capable hands of Roy Thomas Baker.

Thomas Baker, a former Decca trainee classical engineer, joined Trident in 1969, where he'd already contributed to blockbusters like Free's 'All Right Now' and T. 'Get It On' by Rex. His relationship with Queen was difficult, and the resulting finished record lacked structure. Anthony went to Trident to listen to it after returning from Greece, during Thomas Baker's absence, and described what he heard as "schizophrenic."

'So Freddie, Brian, and I came in and remixed most of it. ..'I wanted it to capture the balls and intensity of Queen's live act,' Anthony explained.

The remixes and fine-tuning fatigued everyone involved - as one engineer involved in the project said of Freddie, 'it was pretty nerve-racking dealing with a born celebrity'. Thomas Baker and John Anthony then began visiting labels. Nobody was interested in knowing. It was perplexing. A prevalent critique was that Queen's sound was too overtly reminiscent of bands like Yes and Led Zeppelin, despite the fact that many who worked on the album thought that the Queen sound was distinctive. The band still lacked a record label to print their efforts onto vinyl and distribute their LP. They fared better in terms of music publishing, having earned a deal with B. Feldman and Associates, Inc. Meanwhile, the Sheffields had hired Jack Nelson, a fiery American record industry executive who had perfected his act on the front lines, to assist Queen obtain a record deal and a manager. Nelson would take on the job of Queen manager himself, inspired by what he heard but perplexed by the lack of interest from labels and managers.

'It took me over a year to get a deal with Queen, and everyone turned them down,' Nelson recalled. 'By everyone, I mean everyone. I'm not going to mention names. ..'However, they all know who they are.'

Nelson was astounded by Queen's talent. 'Queen reminded me of The Beatles' make-up,' he would later recall. Each guy was diametrically opposed to the others, the four points of the compass. Mr. Freddie. ..He was classically educated and composed on keyboards. He's a complicated character. Exceptionally gifted. Brian was a rock'n'roll guitarist who brought that impact with him. Exceptionally gifted. Scatter-brained. Focused. He was educated in infrared astronomy. John was the bassist. As bass players do, he brought the solid bit. They were brought back to earth. He graduated with honours with a first-class degree in electronics. Roger, the drummer, held two degrees. They were quite likely the most astute band in the business. And very different personalities - we might walk into an airport and one of us would stop, one would turn right, one would turn left, and one would continue straight on. However, it resulted in a powerful creative force. When they got together in the middle, with the piled vocals, it was incredible.'

Each of them was foremost among equals. Nobody would ever emerge as the pack's leader. Freddie and Roger were partners in crime in terms of their friendship, despite the fact that Roger subsequently remarked that he felt he had more in common with Brian when the band first got together.

'We haven't always gotten along, but we've realised that we need each other,' he told Q magazine in March 2011.

'Brian is my true friend, but I was quite close to Fred. 'I believe we were the bad guys.'

Brian took practically everything too seriously, was patient, contemplative, and obstinate, and rarely gave up control.

'We had quite a sophisticated, multi-way engagement,' he explained to Q. 'That's truly why it worked. In some ways, I was extremely close to Roger because we'd previously been in a band together. We were and still are kind of brothers. We were so similar in our goals and perspectives on music, yet so different in so many other ways. We loved and despised each other like any other pair of brothers. ..In certain ways, I was quite close to Freddie, especially when it came to songwriting. Some of my favourite moments were when I was coaxing Freddie into singing.

What did he and Roger have the biggest disagreements about?

'Anything you can think of. It was included once we got into the specifics of the music. We may dispute for days about a single note.'

John made few comments but made significant contributions, particularly in overseeing the Queen's financial concerns. However, bad humour about songwriting credits would not fade for some years. The revenues went to anyone's name was on the single (including whoever wrote the B-side). Only after all four musicians agreed to credit all tracks to the band as a whole, ensuring that everyone earned equally from each release, did resentment on the matter fade. They wished they had thought of it much sooner. Later, Freddie stated that it was one of the best decisions the band had ever made. Not only is this the most democratic technique, but it also prevents problems from arising. Squabbles over who receives how much have wrecked many a band and friendship, as Freddie's old friend Tony Hadley discovered to his cost. In 1999, he and other Spandau Ballet members John Keeble and Steve Norman filed a lawsuit against principal songwriter Gary Kemp for what they claimed was their due portion of former royalties. They lost, and the band went silent for ten years. They eventually put their disagreements aside to go on a massive return tour in 2009.

Queen's members each brought unique and complimentary influences to the table. Each had a musical talent. While Freddie and Brian were considered the main songwriters, with what appeared to be clashing approaches at times, Roger and John would also write some of the band's greatest songs. Freddie wrote 'Bohemian Rhapsody,' 'Killer Queen,' 'Somebody to Love,' and 'We Are the Champions,' while Brian wrote 'Tie Your Mother Down,' 'We Will Rock You,' 'Hammer to Fall,' and 'Who Wants to Live Forever,' while Roger wrote 'Radio Ga Ga,' 'One Vision,' 'It's a Kind of Magic,' and

'The majority of bands have a front guy and the rest,' says music publicist Bernard Doherty. 'There aren't many bands when four guys take the stage and you go "wow, wow, wow, wow, and wow."'

'Freddie and Brian were totally complementary,' Paul Gambaccini explains. 'Because they did not overlap, there was no reason for jealousy inside the group. Nothing except admiration. They also released each other from any obligation to do what the other did.

Brian May was not a performer. Certainly not in the sense that Freddie was. So Freddie was really convenient for him. Brian could simply stand there and do his job, leaving Freddie to do the rest. At the same time, Brian isn't simply standing there thinking, "I'm a guitar god." He's completely focused on what he's doing, and it's great to watch. Brian was particularly amused by the relative success of the singles written by Freddie, Roger, and John. Compare it to a band like Bread, where David Gates had all the hits and the other authors were ignored by the audience (antagonism between Gates and the late Jimmy Griffin led to Bread's disbandment in 1973). But when it came to Queen, Brian looked to be overjoyed that Freddie's songs were a success. It made for balanced records, which was genius in and of itself.'

After signing their deal with Trident in November 1972, Queen performed for the industry at The Pheasantry, a popular hangout on Chelsea's King's Road from which Bob Geldof would later devise his Live Aid campaign and which, at the time of writing, is a Pizza Express store. Everyone involved had asked for favours, borrowed and stolen address books, filched numbers, phoned about, and requested help from every music industry contact they could think of. Despite all of this effort, the show was poorly attended, and it was a horrible night. The band flagged, the equipment sagged, you name it. Nobody from A&R showed up.

Five days before Christmas, Queen performed at the renowned Marquee Club on Soho's Wardour Street, which had hosted The Rolling Stones in one of their earliest live concerts, in July 1962, and had previously welcomed The Yardbirds, The Who, and Jimi Hendrix. Even though it was an improvement over their dismal night at The Pheasantry, it didn't result in anything like a recording contract. One ray of hope came in the form of Jac Holzman, MD of Elektra Records in the United States. Jack Nelson had handed him tapes of the entire Queen album.

'I listened to them through the speakers first, then through headphones,' Holzman explained later. 'It was recorded and sung so well. Everything was in place, like a neatly cut diamond on your desk. I had been knocked unconscious. "Keep Yourself Alive,"

"Liar," and "The Night Comes Down" are all fantastic songs in a lavish production that felt like the best ice cream poured over a solid rock 'n' roll foundation. 'I desired the Queen.'

Jack Nelson arranged for Jac Holzman to attend the show at The Marquee after lengthy negotiations.

'I flew to London, listened to them at the gig Jack had set up, and was utterly dissatisfied,' Holzman recalled. Nothing on stage matched the power I heard on the tape. But there was music. I sent them a lengthy memo, four or five pages single-spaced, outlining my thoughts and recommendations.'

True, Freddie's camp performance style was still erratic and not to everyone's taste at the time. As an American, Holzman might have expected a more macho and recognizably rock 'n' roll live performance. It's unlikely he expected ballet shoes, feather boas, and leotards. All that balletic posturing and preening seemed at odds with how the band appeared on tape. It simply did not capture Queen's recorded sound in the way that Jac Holzman had hoped.

However, Holzman changed his mind shortly afterwards. After all, he was starting to see what he had heard. Yes, it was unusual and out of the ordinary, but he was warming to it. In America, he agreed to sign Queen to Elektra. Despite the fact that they were about to share a highly regarded American label with The Doors, the band was unable to secure a contract with a UK label. Their unsatisfactory relationship with Trident would continue.

# 9. EMI

Despite the numerous setbacks that led to its creation, Queen's self-titled debut album, released in January 1973, was a masterpiece. They recorded a session for John Peel's progressive radio show the following month. This was a coup in and of itself, because it was virtually unheard of for Radio 1 to record an unsigned band for broadcast at the time. Another lucky break came when Queen's song-publishing company, B. Feldman & Co. was acquired by EMI Music

Publishing, to which the band was automatically signed. This brought them one step closer to realising their dream.

'EMI was the ultimate record label in the Seventies,' says former promotions executive Allan James, who worked for the label before becoming one of the industry's most famous record pluggers. 'Jamesie,' also known to his artists as 'The Man in Black,' has looked after Elton John, Alice Cooper, Rick Wakeman, Kim Wilde, Eurythmics, and countless others over the years.

'Warner and CBS were both American,' Jamesie observes.

'Pye, Decca, and the other UK labels were also unsuccessful. The music industry was represented by EMI Manchester Square. It was also the British filter for American alternative labels like Capitol and Motown at the time. EMI had signed The Beatles, owned every major artist from Vera Lynn to Cliff Richard, and had all of the pop hits. It was the greatest record label in the world in those days, and Queen aspired to be signed by them.

'The Chairman, Sir Joseph Lockwood - the only "sir" in the business at the time - was an outrageously camp figurehead who Freddie idolised. It didn't get much better than Sir Joe. As it turned out, he and Freddie were two peas in a pod, they had so much in common. Delusions of grandeur, for starters: whenever Sir Joseph strode through EMI's reception with his entourage, there was always a lift waiting to take them straight up to his penthouse.

'Then there were the Easts.

'Ken East was EMI's MD in the Seventies. He was this big, bold, brassy Australian who'd been a lorry driver before he got into the music business. Dolly, his wife, used to be in PR. Still was, in many ways. She was a large lady, this irresistible Mama Cass figure. Ken adored artists, and was one of the first to come down from his ivory tower to associate with them. EMI was full of queens, so Ken and Dolly embraced that whole scene too.

'We'd all go out for dinner with Cliff Richard, and make mischief around the Soho clubs. They were Watership Down days, complete make-believe. No wonder Freddie aspired to all that. It was bloody marvellous. As for EMI, why wouldn't they want Queen? That band had EMI written all over them. Why? Because they were so different and intelligent, and had such a creative attitude. They were tuning into the zeitgeist, listening to what music fans wanted, and taking it a step further. They knew what they were doing, and so did EMI.'

The chief A&R man for EMI at the time, and the person who would decide whether the label should sign Queen, was Joop Visser – remembered by former Cockney Rebel frontman Steve Harley as 'a lovely great Dutchman'.

'Joop was the guy who found three of EMI's most successful acts of the era, and signed them all at the same time,' Steve tells me.

'One was Queen. The second was Pilot – the band formed by former Bay City Rollers Billy Lyall (who died of AIDS-related causes in 1989) and Dave Paton. The third, by the way, was us. Joop signed Cockney Rebel for three albums, no options. Not one single with options. No messing about. The kind of deal that is unheard-of now. Joop made my career and changed my life.

'I was twenty-two and full of myself. Thank God I was dealing with Joop; anyone else might have knocked my block off. Joop was the man you deferred to, the one you went to for advice.

'I was my own man, something of a gambler, a bit restless, a bit cocky. But you couldn't offend Joop. I loved him dearly. Maybe I made mistakes that the Queen was smart enough to avoid. Freddie and I had in common a penchant for the theatrical. Not "Glam Rock" in any sense: you wouldn't have called either my band or Freddie's band that. The thing is, Queen fronted by Freddie Mercury would have been theatrical in any era. It didn't need that "Glam Rock" label to validate it or set it in context.'

It was photographer Mick Rock, Steve agrees, who inspired the theatrical bent in artists like Freddie, Bowie and Steve himself.

'And then he pushed it to the hilt. Mick was the catalyst. He was always putting people together. I remember him bringing Mick

Ronson [the late guitarist with Bowie's Spiders from Mars, Mott the Hoople, Van Morrison and many others] round to my flat off the Edgware Road one day, saying that we should meet and that we'd get on like a house on fire. We did, of course. Musos loved Mick. You wanted him down there in the pit, taking the long shots. He was a rock musician who wasn't.

'Mick photographed me everywhere, and did all that great stuff with Queen. He understood me and Freddie, and encouraged us in our creativity. Bands like Queen and Cockney Rebel knew we had to shake the business up. In my heart and soul I'm a folk singer, but at the time I denied all that. Bugger Woodstock. Wearing make-up and poncing around was of its time. I know Freddie felt the same, because we discussed it over dinner down at Legends a few times. I also know they must have loved Joop as much as I did. Especially Freddie.'

It wasn't love at first sight. Visser was seeking a band to fill the gap left by Ian Gillan quitting Deep Purple after their exhausting 'Machine Head' world tour. But the Dutchman was initially unimpressed by the Queen. He too had attended their Marquee Club gig on 20 December 1972, but was underwhelmed. He had watched them in rehearsal, all a bit so-what. He confessed privately that the band members' personalities 'left him cold'. There was work to do.

After another Marquee Club showcase on 9 April 1973, and following three months of complicated negotiations with Trident, during which the latter drove the hardest bargain, refusing to back down, Visser did eventually sign Queen to EMI. It was worth all the agony and the wait. Queen would remain at EMI for the rest of their career . ..almost. (Not until thirty-eight years later, at the end of 2010 and on the eve of remaining band members Brian and Roger entering a year of celebrations for their fortieth anniversary, did Queen abandon the sinking EMI ship to sign with the Universal Music Group. Their recordings have appeared, since January 2011, on the Island Records label.)

Queen's official debut single, 'Keep Yourself Alive' – the opening track of their debut album and written by Brian – was released on 6 July 1973. But they couldn't win. The accompanying promotional blitz was dismissed as 'hype' which, although infuriatingly commonplace in the music business today, was then regarded as opportunistic and in poor taste. Freddie could not have been more frustrated, believing that Queen was doing everything right. Rejected five times by national station Radio 1's playlist programmers, and not yet having the licensed commercial radio stations to fall back on (they only became operational later that year), the track failed to chart. It was both the first and last time in Queen's career that this would occur. The only DJ to give it airtime was the late Alan 'Fluff' Freeman, described by John Peel as 'the greatest out-and-out disc jockey of them all', whose legendary catch-phrase was 'not 'arf', and who played the single on his new Saturday afternoon Rock Show, featuring heavy and progressive sounds.

Undeterred, EMI went into overdrive. Arguably the finest exposure for bands at the time was an appearance on BBC TV's cult rock show The Old Grey Whistle Test, presented by DJ Bob Harris. Its name was inspired from a Tin Pan Alley (community of music publishers and songwriters) term of yore: when virgin pressings of records arrived, executives would give a listen to the 'Old Greys', the doormen in grey suits. Songs that made enough impression to get the old lads whistling the tunes after just one hearing were judged to have passed the 'Old Grey Whistle Test'. Unlike the BBC's Top of the Pops weekly chart show, OGWT featured only album music. The hit programme had been on air for sixteen years, although comparable shows today rarely last a second series.

A 'white label' pressing of Queen's album - a blank LP in a flimsy sleeve – was handed to OGWT's production department. But the plugger had neglected to write the names of the band and record business on the label. No one had any idea who had sent in the disc, nor who the artist was.

'At that time, a lot of the strengths in album music were coming from the States,' recounts OGWT producer Mike Appleton. 'Therefore, most of the bands were not available to come into the studio and play live. To get round that, I created this process whereby I'd choose album tracks and have this great man Phil Jenkinson match the tracks with relevant images. Today, many people claim that this was what led to the birth of the video. And with retrospect, I can conclude that it was all fairly harmful to the music industry. It stole all the money and emphasis away from the live show. Rock venues closed, and eventually all rock TV shows began to look the same.'

Nonetheless, creating the images was a lot of fun.

'Fans started turning into Whistle Tests just to witness those,' Appleton concurred. 'Regular featured musicians included Little Feat, ZZ Top, JJ Cale, early Springsteen, and Lynyrd Skynyrd - I could have played their "Freebird" every week and still received requests for it; that track was the most popular thing at the time. We screened anything from cartoons to abstract flicks to experimental items. It worked fantastically nicely. I picked up this White Label on my desk one day and saw it was unlabeled. I could have disregarded it or thrown it away, but instead I put it on, unaware that it was the first printing of Queen's debut album.'

Appleton was so taken by what he heard that he chose to include the song 'Keep Yourself Alive' on that week's show.

'I called around to attempt to find a name and a source. Nobody knew. Finally, I handed it to Phil and said, 'Let's put this on. We'll state on the show that we don't know what the hell is going on or who the hell is involved, but if anyone out there knows, please call us.' Phil brought in some black-and-white cartoon film of a super silver streamlined train with F.D. Roosevelt's visage on the front, hurtling across America at breakneck speed. The clip had been used in a 1930s political campaign. The following day, EMI called to inform us that the band was Queen, and we intended to announce the audience at the following week's show. But our crowd outdid us. We received an unusually large number of inquiries from ecstatic fans.'

The album was released on July 13, 1973, twelve years before Queen's historic performance at Wembley Stadium for Live Aid. The music press was unimpressed. Most were disdainful of the record at best. Some despised it, particularly New Musical Express writer Nick Kent, who labelled it as "a bucket of urine," resulting in a long-running dispute between Queen and the respected rock weekly. At the very least, the general public was starting to pay attention. The album charted for seventeen weeks, peaking at number twenty-four, and won them a gold disc.

Trident invited Queen into Shepperton Studios to produce new songs and rehearse current material after another session at Radio 1 - with the playlisters still snubbing them. During their time at Shepperton, Queen made their first promotional film, Trident, having recently expanded into video production with another subsidiary company, Trillion. The video, which would accompany the songs 'Keep Yourself Alive' and 'Liar,' would be directed by future film director Mike Mansfield.

'The promo video, then in its infancy, was to become such an integral promotional tool of the music industry that soon record companies would be spending tens of thousands of dollars on top-gun directors, glamorous locations, and dazzling special effects in their efforts to push their artists up the charts,' says Scott Millaney, who produced some of the most iconic pop videos in history, including 'Video Killed the Radio Star' for The Buggles - the first-ever video to be viewed on YouTube. His business, MGMM, would create ten legendary Queen videos in total.

'With all its tactics and strategies, the marketing video business would eventually exhaust itself,' Scott concedes. 'The record industry would then rediscover the human element, and the cycle would start all over again. However, in the 1970s, it was still an exciting and fresh new medium that would considerably enrich the careers of dozens of artists, some of whom did not live up to the hype.'

According to Scott, the effective promo film is built around three key elements: the song's music and lyrics, the 'live' performance, and the artist's distinct imagery. A single broadcast of the video can accomplish more to promote a record and establish an artist than any amount of radio play when the components are just right. As a result, many artists began to abandon the live circuit entirely, realising that a video capture can provide an image of perfection that a live performance can never match.

'The disadvantage is that filming is tough and exhausting,' Scott says.

'Shoots frequently begin at sunrise and may not end until late at night. Artists suffer as a result of their hectic schedules. There's little doubt that companies like ours have elevated video production to the level of an art form. We mined the philosophy to the point that we could tell record companies, "You need to pay a fortune to get the best." At the time, I had the best creative collaborators in the world. We set the benchmark, and we were in operation two years before MTV, which revolutionised everything.'

Queen's initial encounter with the medium was less than positive. The band was uneasy in the studio and clashed with Mansfield, who dismissed most of their 'novice' artistic proposals in favour of his own 'more experienced' ideas. Freddie, in particular, believed that Mansfield was missing the point of Queen's music, and that his efforts were dated, predictable, and 'full of himself'. The outcome was deemed unusable and was abandoned. Queen declined to work with Mansfield on 'Liar' again. They decided that the only way to achieve what they wanted was to make it themselves, so they collaborated with technician Bruce Gowers at London's Brewer Street Studios to develop something 'exactly in sync with the band's own notions of how they should be presented. This unusual clip was the first to be used to promote Queen, yet there were very few outlets on TV in these early days, so it has barely ever been seen till now,' they later said in the accompanying booklet to their DVD collection, Queen Greatest Video Hits 1. Freddie's song 'Liar,' from the same album, was never released as a single in the UK, only in North America, where it was severely edited. The version of the track's promo that appears on the DVD has never been released before.

It had now become clear to the band that they could only relax enough to experiment with their creativity if they maintained near-complete control over their work. This would serve as the blueprint for Queen's whole career.

'I wouldn't say they were control freaks precisely,' Tony Brainsby, Queen's first publicist, told me in 1996, four years before he died. 'However, they always knew exactly what they wanted and found it exceedingly difficult to compromise or make do. It was often fruitless to propose going with something else because they had a perfectly clear sense of how they perceived something.'

Trident hired Brainsby at exorbitant cost to construct Queen's public profile. He made quite a name for himself on the music scene and rode around London in a Rolls-Royce. He was the type of publicist Freddie could connect to: painfully thin, lanky, and bespectacled, and always dressed in a Mandarin-collared black jacket, drainpipe trousers, and Chelsea boots. Brainsby not only had the required post-Swinging Sixties quirky persona, but he also had rock credentials. He shared a Soho flat as a teenager with Eric Clapton and Brian Jones of The Rolling Stones. His Boyfriend magazine column got him to the pop TV show Ready Steady Go! rehearsals on a regular basis., which led him to start his own public relations firm. Brainsby was the most sought-after music publicist in London when he met Queen. He operated his empire from his big, rambling mansion on Edith Grove, between Fulham Road and the King's Road, which was stuffed with dead plants, rock chicks, and an uncountable number of television screens. Those of us who remained recall pitching up there for Brainsby's gatherings and then disappearing for several days.

Mick Rock, a personal friend of Brainsby's, had been his wedding photographer, and his client list included some of the day's biggest acts, from Cat Stevens and Thin Lizzy to Mott the Hoople and The Strawbs.

'The Queen approached Trident through their American manager Jack Nelson,' Brainsby recalled.

'It was unusual for me to take on unknowns. But the Queen was unique. I recall seeing them at Imperial College. There was no stage here, only a dancing floor. Freddie was posing in his white cape and whatever he was wearing. That performance was a far cry from how they finished up. Freddie, on the other hand, had a lot of presence and presentation. He has his act together already.'

What particularly impressed Brainsby was that Freddie did not try to take all the credit.

'What I found admirable was that they never referred to themselves as "Freddie Mercury and Queen." It was always a group photograph.

Freddie never attempted to position himself as the leader. As far as I could tell, the band's relationships were mainly harmonious. They were unique among rock musicians in that they were extremely clever. In their presence, one may feel extremely inadequate.'

Brainsby admitted that at the start of their relationship, Freddie was given more interviews than Brian, Roger, or John.

'Then I learned to make sure they completed an equal amount of work. We'd save Freddie for the big ones later on. Brian was then in charge of the important ones. He'd always spoken about creating his guitar out of an old fireplace, so that was simple, and it got them into the more serious music publications. Roger, the pin-up, did well in teeny girls' magazines like Jackie and 19. He was stunning. At the very least, the band wasn't picky about where they got attention, which was fortunate given how few journalists would give them the time of day. They were, however, quite picky about photos. Before I could distribute anything, they had to personally approve each one. Freddie was the most sensitive of the group. It was all because of his teeth. He was also a stickler for detail. Typical of a Virgo. He'd even designed a coat-of-arms emblem for the band that included all of their star signs.'

All of this foreshadowed Rob Reiner's imaginary heavy metal band, which became the subject of the legendary mockumentary This Is Spinal Tap in 1984.

Brainsby, as cool and laid-back as he was, was immediately attracted by Freddie.

'He had numerous stylish small peculiarities that stuck with you. He'd use black nail polish to paint simply his right or left hand's fingernails. Or he'd just polish one of his tiny fingers. He'd exclaim, "Darling!" or "Dear friends!" every other sentence, and his camp delivery was both hilarious and lovable. He was a pleasure to be around. There is never a dull moment. When he got into the office, the girls were all over it.

'Of course, he was living with Mary at the time. To begin with, his sexual life was a complete mystery to us all; we could never figure it out. He certainly never mentioned it.'

Brainsby never socialised with or became close to any of the members of the band.

'I've never been one to become overly connected with clients. The biggest PR faux pas is mistaking them for your best friends, since they merely take the piss. If you get too close to an artist, they can be a pain in the arse. That sort of thing was left to the girls at my workplace. That is why they were there.'

Rock 'n' roll,' Brainsby concluded, "is an erratic, unstable, emotional, ego-ridden business." The same as its stars. Working in the industry for as long as I have, you learn not to be surprised that nearly every rock artist is a paranoid weirdo. It's what happens to them.'

The fact that Freddie was a charming eccentric was his saving grace.

'I admired him a lot,' Brainsby added. 'Here was a man brimming with creative abilities that were not the result of someone's imagination. They did exist. He knew he had it in him, no matter how old he was. ..I believe it was twenty-seven. They were fairly old for a band to be starting out, after all. He'd carried all of this inside him for a long time. How frustrating it must have been, knowing he had what it took, trying so hard to break into the big leagues and not getting anywhere for so long.'

Freddie had the sense of someone who had understood his full potential from boyhood.

'He was desperate for an outlet for his ideas. Success must have seemed like a huge relief to him. There were times when he had to fight tooth and nail to achieve what he wanted, which did not always bring out the best in him. Having to kick, struggle, yell, punch, and shout to make an impression and get through to people is never easy. That's where I found Freddie when I arrived.'

The most in-demand publicist in London wasn't the only one who had his work cut out for him.

# 10. DUDES

Queen returned to Trident Studios in August 1973 to record their second album.

After Tony Brainsby's tireless efforts raised the band's profile significantly, the band was finally granted its own actual studio time, during daylight hours if they desired.

They gathered at Golders Green Hippodrome on September 13 to record an important session for BBC Radio.

'At Golders Green Hippodrome, we recorded Queen's first live In Concert session, compèred by Alan Black [the late, laconic Scottish DJ, cartoonist, and animator on The Beatles' Yellow Submarine film, who conceived the In Concert series],' recalls BBC producer Jeff Griffin. They did not complete the entire hour. Peter Skellern assisted me. I must concede that it appears to be an odd combo. The Queen was excellent at this. Freddie displayed some uneasiness. Not really surprising, given that they hadn't done much live work. The show was highly received, and there was a lot of attention.'

That same month, their American record label Elektra released the debut Queen album in the United States. After all they'd been through in the UK, the band wasn't expecting much. They were pleasantly pleased, then, when DJs across America lauded them as "an exciting new British talent" and began playing album tracks on the air. A surge in requests propelled the record to the Billboard chart, where it reached at a respectable Number Eighty-Three - no small feat for a relatively unknown band. The accomplishment was not overlooked. Brainsby had already introduced Queen to another fantastic act on his list, Mott the Hoople. The sarcastic, ringlet-haired Ian Hunter fronted Mott. Despite a devoted fan base on the London club scene, their album sales were underwhelming. They'd called it quits in 1972, only to resurface at Bowie's request, when he brought them under his own management. Mott signed a new deal with CBS Records (later Sony), and Bowie composed and produced their hit track 'All the Young Dudes'. Mott had several Top Twenty songs in 1973, including 'All the Way From Memphis' and 'Roll Away the Stone,' prompting a huge UK tour. The tour, which included twenty prime-venue events, began on November 12 in Leeds Town Hall and ended shortly before Christmas at London's Hammersmith Odeon.

The support act was Queen, thanks to Brainsby's introduction and the bung (it was just becoming normal for bands to 'buy' their way into other bands' tours at the time).

Freddie, Brian, and Roger sang backup vocals for Mott on 'All the Young Dudes' on November 1st, at the Kursaal in Southend-on-Sea, the world's first theme park, predating New York's Coney Island.

Maverick Radio Caroline was formed in 1964 as an unauthorised offshore service broadcasting from a ship anchored in international waters off the coast of England. With the self-proclaimed mission of challenging record labels' monopolies and giving the BBC a run for its money in music broadcasting in the UK, it started the careers of many prominent mainstream DJs, including Tony Blackburn, Mike Read, Dave Lee Travis, Johnnie Walker, and Emperor Rosko. Caroline's heyday was cut short by the Marine, &cBroadcasting (Offences) Act 1967, which outlawed pirates in August of that year and jolted the BBC out of its slumber to launch the new 'teenage station', Radio 1, the following month, hosted by Caroline favourite Tony Blackburn. Caroline would return. Meanwhile, as Radio 1 established itself, Radio Luxembourg rose to prominence.

David 'Kid' Jensen joined Luxembourg in 1968, when he was only eighteen years old. The late-night show Kid Jensen's Dimensions, which aired between midnight and three a.m., became one of radio's most popular, gaining a diverse fan base that included British Prime Minister-to-be Tony Blair.

Jensen first met Queen in October 1973, on an EMI-sponsored promotional tour of European cities. As well as France, Germany, Holland and Belgium, the band touched up in the Grand Duchy to deliver a live show coordinated by 'the Kid'.

'From 1968 to 1973, prominent Radio Luxembourg was "the only place in Europe" to hear rock and pop music,' Jensen explains.

'Back then, Radio 1 closed early in the evening, and then it was Radio 2 - at which time many listeners transferred to us. We focused on what was then known as the "progressive" sound. The station was hip, and all of the musicians wanted to be associated with it. I met

Jimi Hendrix's fiancée at a party one night after his death, and she informed me that Jimi enjoyed my act. "We'd come back from parties and listen to you," she went on to say.

'I was captivated with Queen from the start. From their debut album, "Keep Yourself Alive" was the first song I ever heard. I had always preferred guitar-based music, but this was different. It was brimming with vitality. They had it all: John, the quiet, dependable bassist. Brian is a fantastic guitarist. Roger, the superb drummer who revealed his rock-star lifestyle. And then there's Freddie Mercury, the great showman, possibly the best of all time. They'd been turned down despite their amazing recordings and innovative approaches. I knew they hadn't gotten much airplay on Radio 1. When I found out they were on a promotional tour, I scheduled a little gig for them at the Blow Up Club in town, which has a capacity of around 200 people.

'The club's owners, fortunately, took my word for it that the bands I chose were good, so I had some leeway. The crowd was in their late teens and early twenties. It had a varied bill that night, with Queen performing alongside Status Quo, Wishbone Ash, The Grateful Dead, and Canned Heat, among others. This concert was scheduled to be recorded for future transmission by Radio Luxembourg. However, the equipment failed, and there is no record of it. The Queen was confident and boisterous. Even in those early days, he was a cut above the rest.

'After the show, we went back to Freddie's hotel room with their plugger, Eric "Monster" Hall. We stayed up late talking about everything and nothing. Freddie was a terrific host, as he was lively and cheerful. Nothing was too difficult.

'I liked them as humans,' Jensen adds. 'I wrote an article for Record Mirror on them. I respected them for flying in the face of certain critics who did not immediately adore them. They weren't only about sex, drugs, and rock 'n' roll, though they did all of those things. They had an academic air about them. They would have been successful at practically everything, I reasoned. I will be eternally grateful to the Queen for assisting me and my show. I was able to broadcast them late at night on Radio Luxembourg, and they helped me gain a lot of notoriety.'

Their popularity is growing, and the warm-up shows they did for Mott the Hoople's tour were a huge success. Finally, Freddie had what he had always desired: guaranteed audiences, adoration, and people clamouring for more. Rave reviews in the music press were still scarce, with the general impression remaining that Queen were little more than the 'Emperor's New Clothes'.

'Fuck them, sweetie, if they don't get it,' Freddie responded to a perplexed Tony Brainsby.

Tony, who was frequently the target of Freddie's rage and irritation when confronted with negative reviews, couldn't help but see the tremendous effect that fan adoration was having on his charge.

'Despite the negative press, Freddie's confidence skyrocketed. But I could see he didn't like doing interviews. We eventually stopped employing him entirely, unless it was for an album or a tour. Of course, Freddie's deliberate evasiveness only made him appear more mysterious, which attracted him.'

'I suppose, to an extent, we're a sitting target because we've achieved notoriety faster than most bands,' Freddie stated at the time, rewriting history and conveniently forgetting what a long, gruelling, and unpleasant ride it had been to the almost-top. After so much anguish, the falsehood was possibly excusable.

'We've been spoken about more than any other band in the previous month,' he added,'so it's unavoidable. I believe it would be incorrect if we just received positive feedback. But what irritates me is when you receive unfair, dishonest assessments from folks who haven't done their homework.'

Denis O'Regan, the award-winning rock photographer who began his career photographing Bowie at Hammersmith Odeon with a camera borrowed from his uncle, would go on to tour the world with Queen as their official photographer. When he saw them play for Mott at the same location in 1973, he was struck by the lead singer's "pretentiousness and confidence."

'Freddie was throwing shapes and going through the positions even as a basic support act,' Denis recalls.

'In between numbers, he introduced the tunes to the crowd. Brian May was incredible. I'd never heard of Queen, but back then, you went to see the support act as well as the headlining act. "Who does that prat think he is?" I asked my friend George Bodnar (who went on to become a huge figure in rock photography)." Of course, I found out why a year or so later, after the entire world had grown accustomed to the concept of Queen. I first became interested in their music after hearing them on the John Peel show. Since then, I've been a huge Queen fan.'

'For me, it was only after Queen toured with Mott the Hoople that they truly got it together, and I mean shockingly together,' Joop Visser later commented. At the end of that trip, they worried about Mott the Hoople because they were stealing the performances.'

Meanwhile, press reactions were improving. 'Electric atmosphere'. 'A terrific band,' says the press. In Liverpool, Queen completed a watershed moment by backing 10cc.

When asked about the tour that began as Mott's and ended as Queen's, Freddie said, 'The opportunity to play with Mott was amazing. But I knew very well that as soon as we concluded that tour, we'd be headlining in Britain.'


EMI, unable to handle the flood of Queen fan mail and photo requests, attempted to delegate responsibility to Trident Studios. Trident couldn't or wouldn't handle it either. There was only one solution to the dilemma. Queen established its own official fan club by the end of 1973, run by two old friends of Roger's from Cornwall, Sue and Pat Johnstone. While ownership has changed throughout the years, the band has remained actively involved in the club. The fan club not only exists today, but it also organises and stages a well-attended annual Queen Convention.

With album sales on the rise, EMI increased its foreign marketing efforts. In January 1974, a promotional tour to Australia was planned. Following a normal travel inoculation, Brian developed gangrene in his arm that was so severe that amputation was feared. His illness improved quickly enough that the excursion could continue as scheduled. It was then Freddie's time. His phobia of flying first expressed itself on the flight to Sydney, and he grew agitated almost to the point of panic. His anxiousness was aggravated by a terrible ear infection that caused him to lose his hearing temporarily. Freddie would be terrified of flying for the rest of his life. The journey appeared to be cursed. Neither Freddie nor Brian were in the mood to perform, and the shows were a letdown.

Back in London, things were looking up. Queen were awarded the second most promising newcomers in the NME Readers' Poll despite not having a single success to their name. Elektra issued a second album track as a single in America, but it failed to chart. Still undeterred, EMI planned another single release, and when a slot on Top of the Pops became available at the last minute on 21 February 1974 - because David Bowie's promo for his new single 'Rebel Rebel' wasn't ready - Queen were rushed to the BBC studios to mime 'Seven Seas of Rhye', before that single had even been released.

'I remember Freddie running down Oxford Street to catch their performance on a set in a store window since he didn't have a television,' Brainsby recalled.

That week, the single was rushed out, and the tide continued to turn. Queen II, the band's second album, was finally ready for release, and they were organising their first headlining UK tour. It began on March 1 in Blackpool and ended four weeks later at North London's Rainbow Theatre. The building on the corner of Isledon Road and Seven Sisters Road was erected in the 1930s as a theatre but is now Grade II-listed and operated as a Pentecostal church. In the meantime, it was an important music venue: where Jimi Hendrix first lit up his guitar in 1967, where the Beach Boys recorded their Live in London album, and where Stevie Wonder, The Who, Pink Floyd, Van Morrison, The Ramones, and David Bowie performed encores.

The tour's rehearsals began in earnest at Ealing Studios. According to Brainsby, it was Freddie's idea to commission famed young fashion designer Zandra Rhodes to make their colourful tour costumes after seeing some of her creations for Marc Bolan. The others immediately agreed. EMI, not so much, to the eye-watering £5,000 bill, though even they had to admit that Zandra's silk bat-wing tunics were very Queen'. Only now did Freddie feel confident enough to bid farewell to the Kensington Market stall.

Four days after the Blackpool concert, 'Seven Seas of Rhye' debuted at Number 45. Three days later, Queen II was published, reaching number thirty-five despite receiving mixed reviews. The tour was hampered by a number of events, including violence north of the border, where a fight broke out among Stirling University students, resulting in the stabbing of two fans. Despite the fact that the band was able to lock themselves in a kitchen, two roadies were hurt and hospitalised. The following night's event in Birmingham was cancelled, but the damage had already been done. Queen was once again the topic of negative headlines in the music press. The negative publicity persisted after their performance on the Isle of Man at the end of March. Despite this, the band and entourage celebrated the gig in dramatic fashion, raising the bar for post-Queen celebration for years to come. During another event on the tour, the audience began singing 'God Save the Queen' while waiting for the band to appear. From then on, the serenade would be given at Queen concerts.

With Queen II now at number seven on the album chart, more and more people were discovering the first album. That, too, charted for the first time at Number 47, about the same time Elektra released it in Japan, where it was met with ecstasy. Trident, EMI, and the band themselves had no idea how popular Queen would become in Japan.

There was a cost associated with success. There is always something. Job-like Brian began to lose patience as Freddie's anger wore thin and he began to flail at the most minor incident or inconvenience. Their squabbles, which were tiring for everyone, generally culminated in a huffy Freddie flouncing off while the others shrugged. They considered spending time as worthless when there was so much work to be done. Years later, in an interview with the British rock magazine Q to commemorate Queen's fortieth anniversary, Brian and Roger both recalled Freddie as the peacemaker:

'That strikes me as an odd juxtaposition to Freddie's image of being a prima donna. Actually, Freddie was a brilliant diplomat, and if we had disagreements, Freddie was generally able to settle them.'

That beautiful gift called hindsight. Queen, according to Freddie, "argued about everything - even the air we breathe."

Queen, buoyed by the success of their own debut tour, were happy but not shocked to receive an invitation from Mott the Hoople to support their impending US tour, which would begin in Denver, Colorado and conclude with six nights in New York. Despite his fear of flying, Freddie was the first to board the plane on April 12. They'd arrive to find out that Elektra had taken advantage of the band's impending arrival by releasing Queen II ahead of time. They couldn't have been more excited about their first American tour, having worked so hard for it for so long. By this point, the band had piqued the curiosity of some of America's most flamboyant performers.

'We thought we were exceptional,' Brian explained, 'but a lot of the people who came were shocking, even to us - a lot of transvestite artists, The New York Dolls, Andy Warhol - individuals who were innovative in a way that appeared to trash everything that had gone before.'

It was not going to be easy. Brian fainted in New York, having never completely recovered from his sickness in Australia. The band was told they couldn't play in Boston. When Brian got hepatitis, it became clear that they would have to cancel the rest of the tour. His disappointment and shame at having to disappoint the band were palpable.

Despite Brian's continued illness, Queen travelled to the Welsh Rockfield Studios near Monmouth in the Wye Valley to begin rehearsing songs for their third album. In the 1960s, Rockfield was one of the world's first residential recording studios, and it has hosted a diverse range of artists over the last four decades, including Mott the Hoople, Black Sabbath, Motorhead, Simple Minds, Aztec Camera, The Manic Street Preachers, The Darkness (almost a Queen tribute band), and Nigel Kennedy. It was a studio that would become very special to them. On July 15, 1974, they resumed recording at Trident, this time with producer Roy Thomas Baker. Baker, dubbed "the fifth Queenie," had been a Decca engineer in the early 1960s, working with The Rolling Stones, T. Rex, Frank Zappa, and Eric Clapton. He also oversaw albums by Nazareth, Dusty Springfield, and Lindisfarne, among others, making him one of the most well-known producers of the time. Recording, which was split between many London studios other than Trident, particularly Air, Sarm, and Wessex, was abruptly halted when Brian was rushed to the hospital for the second time, this time with a duodenal ulcer. A September trip in the United States had to be cancelled. Brian fell into a deep depression, fearful that Queen would seek a replacement guitarist. He didn't have to be concerned. The rest of the band kept going, recording what they could while leaving space for Brian's guitar sequences to be added later.

Brainsby arranged a clever prank for the presentation ceremony at London's Café Royal, in the shape of comely actress Jeannette Charles. Miss Charles made a living as a double for Her Majesty and had become a national television fixture. She was an inspired choice, especially given that Queen had been working on an inoffensive rock rendition of the British National Anthem to cap future live shows.

The band's third single, 'Killer Queen,' from their impending third album Sheer Heart Attack, was released in October 1974.

Freddie stated at the time, ""Killer Queen" is about a high-class call girl." 'I was trying to suggest that classy people may also be prostitutes,' he said, as if referring to himself. 'That's what the song is about, though I'd like people to put their own spin on it - to read anything they want into it. People are used to Queen's hard-rock intensity, but with that single, you almost expect Noel Coward to sing it. 'It's one of those bowler hat and black suspender numbers,' he remarked, referring to his favourite film, Liza Minnelli's Cabaret. 'Noel Coward would never wear it!"

'It was a watershed moment,' Brian subsequently observed. 'It was the song that best summed up our kind of music, and it was a major hit, and we really needed it as a sign that something successful was occurring for us. We were broke, just like any other struggling rock 'n' roll band. All of them are bedsitters in London, exactly like the rest.'

The blue-eyed heartthrob David Essex, whose hit was ironically titled 'Gonna Make You a Star,' blocked 'Killer Queen' from topping the charts. Queen's next UK tour would be promoted by legendary rock promoter Mel Bush, who had made a star out of none other than. ..Essex, David. The tour was expected to be more grandiose and elaborate than anything Queen had attempted previously. The music press was now compelled to admit that this one-of-a-kind combo could not be dismissed. Not only did Sheer Heart Attack earn rave reviews, but all three Queen albums had debuted on the UK list at the same time.

Another Mick Rock design, the record sleeve artwork, was a departure from the appearance of Queen II.

Freddie told Rock, 'We want to seem like we've been marooned on a desert island.' Rock took him at his word. Rock smeared Vaseline on their faces and nude torsos, then sprayed them with water before laying them down in a circle and shooting them from above. The musical content of the CD was similarly startling, impressing both critics and fans.

'In 1974, my father went out and bought Sheer Heart Attack,' remembers Kim Wilde, daughter of 1950s rock 'n' roller Marty Wilde. Kim would go on to dominate the music landscape during the 1980s, with her debut hit "Kids in America" reaching number two.

'I was fourteen years old and a great pop enthusiast who had just started buying my own records. Slade, Sweet, Mud, Elton John, and Marc Bolan were all favourites of mine. Not to mention The Bay City Rollers - I was fourteen at the time!

'Sheer Heart Attack' is still one of the most thrilling CDs I've ever heard. When the world "went virtual," it was the first record I downloaded on iTunes. I adored Freddie's soaring voice, harmonies, and sense of humour. I really like Brian's guitar playing, which was full of energy and passion, and I had a crush on Roger Taylor. John

Deacon appeared to be the glue that held everything together. What a group!'

They embarked on another UK tour at the end of October, culminating in a single London night at the Rainbow Theatre, which had to be extended to November 19 and 20 when tickets sold out in a matter of days. Both concerts were videotaped and recorded for posterity and future distribution. Promoter Mel Bush presented the band with a plaque in celebration of their having sold out the whole tour at Queen's debut end-of-tour party, held at the Swiss Cottage Holiday Inn and remarkably decent by future standards. Their first European dates were slated for the end of November in Scandinavia, Belgium, Germany, and Spain. Continental album sales were off the charts, and the majority of the shows were sold out. The 6,000-seat venue in Barcelona, a place Freddie fell in love with and would return to again and again, was sold out in twenty-four hours.

By December, Queen had concluded that their relationship with Trident was no longer viable. With the popularity of Sheer Heart Attack, their earnings had increased from £20 to £60 per week, but it was still insufficient to live on. Worse, despite anticipated royalties, Trident declined to provide an advance. Trident refused to lend John Deacon the £4,000 deposit he needed to buy a small house for himself and his expectant partner, Veronica Tetzlaff. Roger desired a little automobile, whereas Freddie desired a new piano. All cash requests were flatly declined. Relations had become so strained that it was decided to hire a specialist music business lawyer to sort out the situation. Queen's association began with Henry James 'Jim' Beach, the senior music partner at Harbottle & Lewis. In 1978, he was appointed manager, a post he still holds today. It would take him nine months to work out Queen's many written agreements with Trident, who understandably wanted to keep the band. Meanwhile, with both the single 'Killer Queen' and the album Sheer Heart Attack charting in the United States, they were deemed fit to embark on their own major US tour.

On January 18, 1975, John married Veronica, with whom he had six children. The band left for their huge US tour on February 5th. Again, despite enthusiastic support from their American label

Elektra, they ran into trouble, with critics drawing comparisons to Led Zeppelin. Freddie had his first voice troubles after developing - or not, depending on differing diagnosis - non-malignant throat nodules. Disobeying doctors' directions to remain silent for three months - absurd! - He strode out in full voice the next night in Washington. Queen had no choice but to cancel numerous booked US gigs as his condition worsened one moment and improved the next. What was becoming clear was that Freddie was giving too much on stage. His performances were too much for his physique and voice chords. He needed time away from touring and recording to heal. It took some time for Freddie and the band to grasp this.

There were additional fortunate escapes. While on tour in the United States, Queen agreed to meet with the feared Don Arden, the former Brixton-based Vaudeville-era nightclub singer and comedian Harry Levy, with the intention of hiring him as their manager if he could get them out of their debilitating Trident arrangement. They had to be desperate. The late music manager and agent who famously oversaw the careers of the Small Faces, ELO, and Black Sabbath was dubbed 'the English Godfather' due to his aggressive and unlawful financial operations. When discussions did not go his way, Arden was known to resort to violence. According to legend, he even hanged artists from upper-floor windows to get them to sign on the dotted line. Arden became Ozzy Osbourne's father-in-law when his daughter Sharon married Black Sabbath's frontman. To think that Queen may have fallen under the grip of rock's Al Capone. ..Would any of them have survived?

## 11. RHAPSODY

The Queen was completely unprepared for the 'Beatlemania' that greeted them in Tokyo in April 1975. More than 3,000 ecstatic fans jammed into Haneda International Airport's arrivals area, many of them waving homemade banners and Queen discs. With Sheer Heart Attack and 'Killer Queen' both at the top of the charts and every Japan show sold out months in advance, their heroes' reception should have come as no surprise. Perhaps it didn't, according to

Freddie, who rose to the occasion magnificently, waving and smiling gleefully. One reporter remarked that he presumably felt so at ease there because he didn't have to hide his buck teeth, which appeared to be common among Japanese fans. He was enthralled not only by their hordes of fans, but also by the area itself. What better place to reawaken his dormant sense of the unusual - especially to someone distanced and estranged from his own? Everything about Japan, from its history, traditions, and culture to its advanced technology lifestyle, captivated him. He quickly developed an interest in Japanese pottery, paintings, and other works of art.

The country and the man shared many similarities. Japan, like Freddie, was a jumble of contradictions: an ancient curiosity with a complicated, varied personality. The names of her thousand islands reverberated like magic spells in his mind: Hokkaido, Honshu, Kyushu, and Shikoku. He was intrigued by the polite and stoic Japanese, who had weathered decades of feudal oppression to emerge from WWII with such calm. Freddie dashed around, taking in everything. He ate sushi and sake while bartering for dolls, silk kimonos, and lacquer boxes. He frequented the infamous bath-houses and kage-me-jaya ('shadow teahouses' popularised by American GIs), and hung out with both types of geishas. He encountered Akihiro Miwa, a stunning drag queen who created and directed his own cabaret on Tokyo's Ginza (Paris' Pigalle or London's Soho). Following Freddie's initial visit, Miwa (at the age of seventy-five, still sporting bright yellow shoulder-length hair) began singing Queen songs in honour of his new companion.

'The one time Freddie was a classic tourist was in Japan,' his PA Peter Freestone said afterward. 'Things Japanese were an all-consuming obsession for him, but anywhere else in the world he stayed was just a bed for the night.'

Queen's first and final tour gigs, both at Tokyo's Nippon Budokan Hall, were legendary. Even the bulk of their Sumo wrestler security guards couldn't keep a 10,000-strong swarm of frightened teenaged girls at bay. At one point during the first act, Freddie was obliged to call a halt to ask the audience to take deep breaths and relax for their own safety. Every city they visited had the same tale.

On their return to the UK, they received both good and bad news. The band were still weathering the Trident storm, despite being the toast of the exasperatingly fickle British media, with an Ivor Novello and a Belgian Golden Lion Award for 'Killer Queen' to their names. According to the Sheffields, they had invested more than £200,000 in a new band. Sheer Heart Attack alone had cost £30,000 to produce - little in today's terms, but extravagant at the time. They anticipated to start earning a profit now that they were getting hits, but instead discovered that they still owed Trident a small sum. The Queen found it terrible that they appeared to the outside world to have made it yet were still broken. Their only option was to knuckle down and start writing new songs for another album. The procedure was fraught with tension as they began to vent their emotions on one another, fueling rumours that they had decided to split up. Such a rumour was exactly what the Queen needed to make them see reason and agree to a truce. They were all in it together. Trident negotiated an agreement under which the band would be released from their contracts in exchange for a £100,000 one-time payment and a 1% royalty on the next six albums. They didn't have the money to resolve this at the moment. They could now sign new deals with EMI Records UK and Elektra USA, and they'd get by with a little help from their friends.

Queen rehearsed tracks for their fourth album, A Night at the Opera, in a rented house in Herefordshire in August 1975. The title was taken from a comedy film by the Marx Brothers, which had been a hit in 1935 and which Queen adored. They then decamped back to Rockfield, which would acquire legendary status as the studios used for the backing track of 'Bohemian Rhapsody'. When Freddie pitched up with it, recalled Brian, 'He seemed to have the whole thing worked out in his head.'

The song, an epic undertaking comprising an a cappella introduction, an instrumental sequence of piano, guitar, bass and drums, a mock-operatic interlude and a loaded rock conclusion, at first seemed insurmountable.

'We were all a bit mystified as to how he was going to link all these pieces,' said Brian.

The song brought to life a host of obscure classical characters: Scaramouche, a clown from the commedia dell'arte; astronomer Galileo; Figaro, the principal character in Beaumarchais' The Barber of Seville, and The Marriage of Figaro, from which operas by Paisiello, Rossini and Mozart had been composed; Beelzebub: identified in the Christian New Testament as Satan, Prince of Demons, but in Arabic as 'Lord of the Flies', or 'Lord of the heavenly dwelling'. Also in Arabic, the word 'bismillah', which is a noun from a phrase in the Qur'an: 'bismi-llahi r-rahmani r-rahim', meaning 'in the name of God, most gracious, most merciful'.

I once presented my own theory about these figures from 'Bohemian Rhapsody' to Freddie at a party in his hotel suite in Budapest in 1986. Scaramouche had to be the real Freddie, didn't he? His return to the tearful-clown theme in his songwriting (Pagliacci in 'It's a Hard Life') hinted at what was to come. Galileo Galilei, the sixteenth-century astronomer, mathematician, physicist, and father of modern science, undoubtedly represented scholarly Brian. Beelzebub was clearly Roger, Queen's wildest party animal, with 'a devil put aside' for his pal. I was ironically referring to John, "the shy one," as Figaro - not the operatic character, but the tuxedo kitten from Disney's 1940 animated feature film Pinocchio. Freddie, on the other hand, adored his cats. Perhaps not. ..However, as Freddie stated, all theories are welcome. He'd never revealed anything about the meaning of 'Bo Rap,' even telling his DJ pal Kenny Everett that it was "random rhyming nonsense." So why would he tell me the truth? I didn't think he'd do it. He stared at me for a moment before responding with a Mona Lisa smile.

That seemingly endless recording process took its toll on all concerned – not least, thanks to the layering and overlaying of endless vocals, on the actual tape.

'People think it's this legendary story,' said Brian, 'but you could hold the tape up to the light and see through it . ..every time Freddie added another "Galileo", we lost something'.

At Sarm East and Scorpio Studios in London, a feast of overdubbing began. This was not without incident, as friend and former artist Robert Lee recalls.

'I had just started recording as part of Levinsky/Sinclair [a duo signed to Tony Stratton-Smith's Charisma, familiar from The Kenny Everett Show],' says Lee, who now edits The Who's official website.

'Freddie was friendly with a flatmate of mine, and we used to go antique shopping on a Friday morning in Portobello. I remember he always had impeccable taste: I still have two Chinese prints he insisted I buy when I was looking for a present for my mum . ..I nicked them back after she passed away.

John Sinclair – now a rabbi living in Jerusalem – owned Sarm Studios at the end of Brick Lane. His sister Jill was there, bless her.' (She has since suffered a tragic accident.)

'Queen were in, mixing "Bohemian Rhapsody". Roy Thomas Baker at the helm. Freddie and co. at the desk. It was a twenty-four-track mega-mix, involving slave reels [bearing submixes of tracks from a master reel, to record overdubs against], pre-mixes, and rehearsals for the mix. So many faders had to be precisely cued, it was really tricky. They spent hours and hours trying to get it right, never quite succeeding. And then, miracle, this was the one. Everything was going perfectly. They were getting through it, nearly at the end. Everyone was tense with adrenalin, but very happy. And then, suddenly, the lights went out . ..and in walks Jill, proudly carrying a huge cake aglow with candles, and she was singing "Happy Birthday dear Freddie, Happy Birthday to you!" and they had to start all over again . ..'

'Is this the real life . ..is this just Battersea,' sings Allan James with a smile. '"Bohemian Rhapsody" was parodied from day one: the sincerest form of flattery. Queen changed everything with a six-minute single.'

'The recording was a sheer work of art,' says Searchers bass player Frank Allen, 'over and above what most other outfits were offering at the time. The way they layered their pieces at a time when we had only reached twenty-four analogue track machines, a lot back then but remarkably modest and limiting now, was so impressive, and of course culminated in their tour de force, "Bohemian Rhapsody". Even now it is mind-boggling how they achieved it. Every new layer of harmony meant a degeneration of sound quality, and the gap between brilliance and disaster was alarmingly narrow. They came away with brilliance in spades.'

It was not obvious at the time how much Freddie Mercury and Elton John had in common. Little did they know, in 1975, that Elton would be one of the last to hold Freddie's hand as he lay dying sixteen years later.

They had first met, briefly, in the late 1960s, when Freddie saw the then-little-known singing pianist perform at the famous Crawdaddy Club in Richmond, Surrey. The club was known around the world for hosting top American blues acts, and for its support of The Rolling Stones. Launched by filmmaker Giorgio Gomelsky at the end of 1962, it was originally located at the Station Hotel opposite Richmond railway station. It later moved to the local athletic ground to accommodate more fans. The Crawdaddy had staged early shows by Eric Clapton with The Yardbirds, Led Zeppelin and Rod Stewart, and was precisely the kind of venue to which Freddie aspired. That was something to dream about when he started sitting as a naked life model in his college's Art evening class for ten years a week.

To those on intimate terms with both Elton and Freddie, there were uncanny similarities. Both, in boyhood, had been devoted to their mothers. Both had been reclusive, sensitive children who had taken piano lessons from an early age. Both had changed their names – Elton from Reginald Kenneth Dwight to Elton Hercules John; like Freddie, he had picked the name of a mythological Roman god. Elton's road to stardom had also been long, winding and obstacle-strewn. Each had been at odds with his looks, and had developed an outlandish style – in Elton's case eccentric spectacles, platform boots, feathered and fringed outfits – to disguise his self-perceived ugliness. Each was confused to say the least about his sexuality.

James Saez, a musician, producer and engineer in Los Angeles who has worked with Madonna, Led Zeppelin, Radiohead and Red Hot Chili Peppers, believes that sexuality was the key to both Elton's and Freddie's artistry.

'Was there any bigger struggle than being a homosexual in the Seventies and trying to expose yourself without, well, exposing yourself?' wonders James.

'It seems pretty plausible that Elton created a whole persona for himself, which was full of costumes and theatrics, in order to handle this dilemma and still open himself up. I would assume that "Farrokh" was dealing with similar struggles. The thing that always cut me about him was that as strong and charismatically flamboyant as Freddie looked, he still somehow seemed really fragile and almost innocent.'

For Elton, as for Freddie, there had been girlfriends, and what looked to the outside world like conventional romance. German recording engineer Renate Blauel is said to remain heartbroken by the failure of her brief marriage to Elton in 1984. He has been openly gay since 1988, and entered a civil partnership with filmmaker David Furnish in 2005; they have a son, Zachary Jackson Levon Furnish-John, born to a surrogate mother on Christmas Day 2010.

Freddie's and Elton's personalities developed in parallel, and they grew to depend on each other's friendship.

'Elton's a good old cookie, isn't he?' remarked Freddie. 'I love him to death and I think he's fabulous. To me, he's like one of those last Hollywood actresses of any worth. He has been a pioneer in rock 'n' roll. The first time I met him he was wonderful, one of those people you can instantly get on with. He said he liked "Killer Queen", and anyone who says that goes in my white book. My black book is bursting at the seams!'

But a more tragic dimension to their similarities would soon emerge. As one psychoanalyst would say of Elton in 'Tantrums & Tiaras', the TV documentary produced by David Furnish, 'He was born an addict. He is a totally obsessive-compulsive person. If it hadn't been alcohol, it would have been drugs. If it hadn't been drugs, it would have been food. If it hadn't been food, it would have been relationships. And if it hadn't been relationships, it would have been shopping. And you know what, I think he's got all five.' It was a verdict with which Elton himself did not disagree. As a result of his courage in allowing these views to be aired, the singer experienced an enormous upsurge in public support. It was a virtual mirror image of the person Freddie became in the mid-Eighties, when fame and all its diversions took their toll.

In 1975, the most significant thing the pair had in common was a feisty Scot named John Reid.

The twenty-six-year-old Paisley-born impresario, a power-hungry mogul controlling a business worth £40 million, had arrived via a circuitous route. Having worked in a men's outfitter's, his first job in the music business was as a record plugger. Socially-ambitious Reid had risen through the ranks, cultivated high-profile friendships, and was Elton's live-in lover for around five years, becoming his manager when Reid was still only twenty-one. Reid was another man who dithered over his sexuality: by 1976 he had switched sides, if only briefly, and was engaged to teenaged Sarah Forbes, a publicist from his own Rocket Records office. Sarah is the daughter of film director Bryan Forbes and actress Nanette Newman. She did survive the fall-out, and went on to marry actor John Standing (aka Sir John Ronald Leon Standing, fourth Baronet of Bletchley Park). Reid's business relationship with Elton survived for twenty-eight years, but ended acrimoniously. In 2000, Elton began a multimillion pound High Court battle against Reid, claiming mishandling of business affairs.

Also in 1975, Elton teamed up with a second Scot carving a name for himself: Rod Stewart. Both had worked with Long John Baldry, and had agreed to co-produce an album designed to revive Baldry's flagging career. It was during sessions for this LP that they hit upon the old theatrical custom of calling themselves by women's names. Elton was dubbed Sharon Cavendish, a name which he would use routinely on tour. Rod was Phyllis, after the actress Phyllis Diller. Baldry became Ada, and John Reid was Beryl, in homage to British actress Beryl Reid. When Freddie found out, he had to join in, and became Melina, after Greek actress Melina Mercouri. Cliff Richard, because of the vast number of framed records he'd been awarded down the decades, was Silvia Disc. Neil Sedaka, for similar reasons, was Golda Disc. Freddie would one day employ an entire entourage known by female names. His PA was Phoebe (Peter Freestone), his former lover turned chef was Liza (Joe Fanelli), and his personal manager Paul Prenter was Trixie. Nor were friends and band members immune: Brian was Maggie, as in Rod's hit 'Maggie May'. Roger was Liz, for Elizabeth Taylor. David Nutter, brother of famous tailor Tommy Nutter, was Dawn, and Mick Jagger's assistant and Freddie's long-standing friend, Tony King, became Joy. Mary Austin, taking things the other way, was Steve, as in TV's The Six Million Dollar Man, Steve Austin. Did she mind?

'Nobody was allowed to mind!' laughed Phoebe. 'You knew that someone was accepted if they got "a name". John Deacon never had one, curiously. Perhaps because he was so shy.'

With Elton in self-imposed semi-retirement after an arduous six-year global slog, John Reid, now running Elton's own label, Rocket Records, as well as managing the star, was keen to expand his empire. He jumped, inevitably, at the chance of managing the Queen. Although the band had other possible managers in their sights – Led Zeppelin's Peter Grant, The Who's tour manager Peter Rudge and 10cc's Harvey Lisberg among them – a process of elimination led to Reid getting the gig. It was not what anyone would have called ideal, despite the fact that Reid's first, impressive move was to raise the £100,000 necessary for the band to pay off Trident. He did this simply by going to EMI for an advance against future publishing royalties.

Elton denounced it to their mutual manager as a sure-fire flop. EMI and the industry in general voiced misgivings. Radio stations wondered what the hell they were supposed to do with a six-minute single. Even bassist John Deacon expressed his fears, albeit in private, that to release 'Bohemian Rhapsody' would prove the greatest error of judgement of Queen's career. For a song that was to enter the annals of music history as the all-time rock classic, it had the shakiest of stars. Even those who recognised its magnificence immediately were reluctant to go on record, so dramatic was the departure of 'Bohemian Rhapsody' from any previously accepted convention of rock.

Who knew what really ignited Freddie's imagination and inspired him to create this song? Soaring and decadent, brimming with thinly-disguised personal agony and ecstasy, it is an impossible blend of baroque and ballad, of Music Hall and monster rock. Its incongruous elements are held together by a string of cacophonic guitar-grindings, classical piano sequences, sweeping orchestral arrangements and rich, multifaceted chorales, all dubbed, overdubbed and overdubbed again to the point that, depending on one's mood, it can be unbearable to listen to. There can be few rock fans on the planet who don't know it by heart.

'Even though it was the most amazing piece of work, revolutionary and incredible, I'm so bored with it now,' admits Radio 2 producer and record collector Phil Swern.

'It comes up with alarming regularity on playlists, and it is pretty well played to death. Still, no one could deny what an outstandingly clever piece of work it is. Nearly six minutes long, and it broke every rule. What comes close? Always The Beatles: "A Day in the Life" (the final track on their 1967 album Sgt Pepper's Lonely Hearts Club Band, 5.03 minutes). Led Zeppelin's "Stairway to Heaven" (8.02 minutes, and the most requested song on FM radio shows in the States, although it was never released as a single there). And "McArthur Park" (7.21 minutes) by Jimmy Webb and recorded by Richard Harris.'

'Get far enough away from it and perspective changes everything,' points out Paul Gambaccini.

'It's hard to get excited today about your three-and-a-half-minute rock song or pop record when lengthy masterpieces like "Bohemian Rhapsody", "McArthur Park", "Hey Jude", "Light My Fire" and "American Pie" have already been made. No one aspires to that level of musical achievement any more. We can now look back on these works as artistic achievements of the highest order. Don McLean didn't make "American Pie" to be a single, because he couldn't imagine it was possible for it to be a single. It was eight and a half minutes long. It was the record company who divided it in two. Don was a pure artist who couldn't even have conceived "American Pie" as a hit. It was clearly a masterpiece, but he recorded it as one long album track. The same goes for "Bohemian Rhapsody", which was the last track on Queen's 1975 album A Night at the Opera.

'OK, yes, Freddie wrote the song,' adds Paul, 'but Brian did that incredible guitar passage in the middle, Roger did the high notes, and John contributed, of course. To spread out the contributions in that way is fantastic, as they would later do with their own individual compositions, and I'm sure it's what helped keep them going as a group. It took the genius of Kenny Everett to hear and see "Bohemian Rhapsody" as a classic single.'

Everett, known as 'Ev', a close friend of Freddie's, was a Merseyside-born former Radio Luxembourg presenter and friend of The Beatles, who made his name as a Radio 1 DJ, and as presenter and comedian of his own Kenny Everett Video and Kenny Everett Television shows. He was diagnosed with HIV in 1989, and died of AIDS complications in 1995, aged fifty. In 1966, Ev married former pop singer 'Lady Lee' Middleton, singer Billy Fury's former girlfriend, who would eventually become the psychic and spiritual healer Lee Everett Alkin. The couple separated in 1979, when Everett came out. It is widely believed that he was infected by his promiscuous Russian lover Nikolai Grishanovitch, who was infamous in gay circles ('that careless twat Nikolai') for having done more to spread HIV around London during the early 1980s than any other individual. A former Red Army soldier who succumbed to the disease himself in 1990, Grishanovitch is sometimes named as the person who infected Freddie – although several people I spoke to believe it was the late Ronnie Fisher, a former CBS/Sony publicist.

'I don't think the dates fit on the "Nikolai-infected-Freddie" theory,' reasons Paul Gambaccini.

'I don't recall meeting Nikolai until the year [1987] the government made the original AIDS-awareness ads – because I remember meeting him with Freddie when the ads were about to come out. Freddie showed his first symptoms within one or two years of this. Bearing in mind that the average time between infection and onset of symptoms was ten years, this is just too short a time. Besides, I knew Freddie had been what our parents would have called "loose" since the late Seventies, which is a perfect match for the ten-year average. It's not impossible that it was Nikolai . ..but really unlikely.

'I don't know where Freddie and Nikolai met,' adds Paul, 'but I would not have been surprised if it had been at the Coleherne in Earl's Court. This was one of Freddie's favourite pubs [the other being the London Apprentice in Shoreditch], and had the distinction of being within walking distance of Freddie's home. This was the pub in which it is commonly assumed HIV was introduced to London by an American visitor. His entire circle fell to the disease.'

As 'Ev' and Freddie were movers and shakers on the same gay and music business scenes, it was inevitable that their paths would cross.

'I never thought that Freddie and Kenny were lovers,' says Paul. 'Had they been, I would have thought that everyone in our circle would have known. The reason I never entertained the thought they were is because their sexual personae were too similar. Of course, that means nothing in terms of one-nighters amongst two curious persons, but the idea just doesn't gain traction in my head. To be blunt, they were just silly together.'

Everett played a pivotal role in getting 'Bohemian Rhapsody' released as a single, and was famously first to air the track. A demo was sent to him with strict instructions not to broadcast it, but simply to get back to Freddie with his opinion. Everett adored the track, and played it fourteen times over one weekend, claiming to his boss on every play that 'his finger slipped'. While his cheek helped bring the most popular track of all time to the attention of the metropolis, it is disputed as to whether he made it a nationwide hit.

'In 1975 I had my own daily Radio 1 show,' says "Diddy" David Hamilton, of his hugely popular programme which attracted sixteen million listeners daily.

'The line-up was Noel Edmonds on the Breakfast Show, Tony Blackburn mid-morning, Johnnie Walker over lunch, me after lunch. We'd all have our Record of the Week. It would obviously have been very easy to pick Abba or the Bee Gees, as all their singles were automatically hits. But sometimes you'd think outside the box. That October, along came the well-known record plugger Eric Hall to see me.

'I was living in a flat in Hallam Street behind BBC Broadcasting House, and I'd often get records dropped off to me at home,' remembers Diddy.

'Eric turned up this particular day with "Bohemian Rhapsody", going "Monster! Monster! This could be a big hit!" When I listened to it, I remember thinking that it was totally different from any pop record I'd ever heard before. It was innovative. Operatic. It soared and swooped and got under your skin. You couldn't stop humming bits of it. It got very mixed reviews in the office. Tony Blackburn said he didn't understand it. No one else seemed to like it very much. Compared to the disco sound going down at the time – K.C. and the Sunshine Band's "That's the Way I Like It" and all that – it was unique. The Queens were so different. The Stones were a traditional rock band. This band could rock, but they were not essentially rockers. There is a difference.

'I told my producer Paul Williams that I wanted it as my "Hamilton Hotshot". He agreed. The record, of course, went on to be Number One for a record nine weeks, and by January 1976 had sold more than a million here, was a multimillion seller all over the world, and is arguably the greatest pop song of all time. I like to think that I played my part in that. I was always very proud of my Hotshot choices, and that one didn't let me down. Much has been made over the years of Kenny Everett having stolen a copy of the single ahead of release, playing it endlessly on Capital Radio, and then claiming that he introduced it to the world. He gave it enormous backing, and then took a lot of the credit for it having become a hit. But Capital was in those days exclusively a London station. Nobody else in the UK was hearing it at that time. Radio 1 never got the credit for bringing the single to the attention of the nation!'

The single would reach Number One again for five weeks in 1991, when it was re-released following Freddie's death. It became the UK's third best-selling single of all time, and topped charts around the world. In the US, the record made Number Nine in 1976, and then returned to the chart there in 1992 thanks to the massive popularity of the movie Wayne's World, which famously paid homage to 'Bohemian Rhapsody'.

The late Tommy Vance, one of the biggest names in rock broadcasting, with shows on London's Capital, Radio 1, Virgin Radio and VH-1 rock TV for MTV, described 'Bohemian Rhapsody' as 'the rock equivalent of the assassination of JFK'.

'We all remembered what we were doing when we first heard it,' he told me. 'I was doing the weekend rock show on Capital at the time. I heard it and thought it was a lunatic asylum of a pop song. It was so magnificently obscure, it had to make it. Technically, the song's a mess. It follows no known conventional nor commercial formula. It is just a string of dreams, flashbacks, flash-forwards, vignettes, completely disjointed ideas. It changes sequence, colour, tone, tempo, all for no apparent reason – which is exactly what opera does. But the intent was remarkable. It was the ultimate optimism. It had an indefinable quality, some remarkable magic. It is brilliant. And it is still revered as an icon today. What other song stands up against it? Absolutely fuck all. But try to dissect "Bohemian Rhapsody" lyrics, and you'll find that it's meaningless.'

Oscar-winning lyricist Sir Tim Rice, co-creator of some of the greatest shows in stage-musical history, including Joseph and the Amazing Technicolour Dreamcoat, Jesus Christ, Superstar and Evita – and co-writer of songs with Freddie for the 1988 Montserrat Caballé extravaganza Barcelona, begs to differ.

'It's fairly obvious to me that this was Freddie's "coming-out song",' he tells me.

'I've even spoken to Roger about it. I heard the record very early on, and it struck me that there is a very clear message contained in it. This is Freddie saying "I'm coming out. I'm admitting that I'm gay."

'Yes, he was admitting his homosexuality to himself initially . ..but then, by default, to the rest of the world, because it was such a huge hit everywhere. "Mama, I just killed a man . .." He's killed the old Freddie he was trying to be: the former image. "Put a gun against his head, pull my trigger, now he's dead" – he's dead, the "straight" person he was originally. "Mama, life had just begun, but now I've gone and thrown it all away . .." I mean, this is just my theory, but it does fit. He's shot and destroyed the man he was trying to be, and now this is him, trying to live with the new Freddie. It's very obscure, of course. But think about that middle bit: "I see a little silhouetto of a man . .." That's him, still being haunted by what he's done and what he is. It works for me. Every time I hear the record on the radio, I think of him trying to shake off one Freddie and embracing another – even all these years after his death. Do I think he managed it? I think he was in the process of managing it, rather well. Freddie was an exceptional lyricist, and "Bohemian Rhapsody" is beyond any doubt one of the great pieces of music of the twentieth century.'

An echo, then, of the song's composer himself? Freddie resolutely avoided explanations.

'Does it mean this, does it mean that, is all anybody wants to know,' Freddie sighed. 'Fuck them, darling. I will say no more than what any decent poet would tell you if you dared ask him to analyse his work: if you see it, dear, then it's there.'

As far as Brian was concerned, it was vital that the song's meaning remain obscure.

'I don't think we'll ever know, and if I knew I probably wouldn't want to tell you anyway,' he said.

'I certainly don't tell people what my songs are about. I find that it destroys them in a way, because the great thing about a great song is that you relate it to your own personal experiences in your own life. I think that Freddie was certainly battling with problems in his personal life, which he might have decided to put into the song himself. He was certainly looking at recreating himself. But I don't think at that point in time it was the best thing to do, so he actually decided to do it later.'

I believe Brian meant that Freddie was resisting the inevitable: having to end his relationship with Mary to start a new life as a homosexual. But the thought of doing so terrified him, so he kept putting it off – not least because he dreaded the effect it would have on his parents. Coming out could have made his life so much easier in the long run, as it had for Kenny Everett, who alienated neither his fans nor his wife with his honesty. As Lee Everett told me, 'He was what he was. Didn't stop me loving him. We remained devoted to each other until the end.'

'Had Freddie come out to the world, it would have been as if no one else was coming out,' points out Simon Napier-Bell.

'It wouldn't have been like George Michael, who only came out when he was forced to, and anyway wasn't really a rock star, just high-class pop. Had Freddie come out, he would have rubbed homophobe noses in their own hypocrisy, and it would have been a smaller step than he thought – because to all his friends he was already out, and outrageous.

'When he said he was different in his private life from the performer he was on stage, what he really meant was that he was forced to retire into his shell because of the fear his Parsee family would have had of him coming out. Had he come out from the beginning, his long, slow death would have been something that the gay community could have thanked him for. They would have used it to their advantage, turned it into something wonderfully, tragically showbusiness, and made him the new Judy Garland. He might even have found himself enjoying it!'

'Bohemian Rhapsody' may well have been an allegory of the new, liberated Freddie killing the old persona and revelling in his true self, once hidden but at last revealed, according to The Searchers' bassist Frank Allen:

'But it might be something entirely different. I am not privy to the information, and I never asked him. When Don McLean was asked about the meaning of "American Pie", he replied, "It means I don't ever have to work again." Perhaps the reality of "Bohemian Rhapsody" contains a comparably innocent and more direct truth. I'm not clever enough to judge. I am content just to enjoy it as a beautifully-constructed major work in pop music. Magnificently assembled, it resulted in a three-piece suite of different time signatures and moods that approximated the great classics. In a pop sense, it worked in a way that no one had experienced ever before.'

As Tommy Vance pointed out, what really proved the worth of 'Bohemian Rhapsody' was neither its ground-breaking lyrics nor those brain-scrambling melodies. No amount of speculation as to its meaning, nor even unprecedented airplay, made it a hit. What did so was television.

## 12. FAME

'It was the first smash generated by a picture,' says Allan James, a veteran record promoter. 'Previously, The Beatles' visuals and so on were just fun little videos to accompany the tracks. Nobody ever figured out how to take the Queen. It was the footage that finally broke them. After that, they could no longer be dismissed as a quirky camp rock band. They steered the entire industry in a different path.'

'The chart success of "Bohemian Rhapsody" pushed Top of the Pops to give it a shot,' DJ Tommy Vance recalled. 'Because if a record made the Top Thirty, they had to play it. The more they played it, the higher it rose in the charts. What was truly amazing was that the video, directed by Bruce Gowers and produced by Lexi Godfrey for Jon Roseman Productions, was shot for only £5,000!'

The video helped Gowers, who went on to direct American Idol on television. Gowers became the go-to producer-director for music and comedy specials, working with Michael Jackson, The Rolling Stones, Paul McCartney, Britney Spears, Robin Williams, Billy Crystal, and Eddie Murphy, among others.

'Gowers was doing a performance video with the band at Elstree and shot the video for "Bohemian Rhapsody" in four hours on the same day,' Vance remembered. It was truly inventive. Long before electronics and computers, he employed prisms to generate certain visual effects. Where did he receive his inspiration? The song had an impact on him. It was a conglomeration of so many exciting ideas that Bruce's ideas just flowed. The basic concept, however, was based on a prior record cover, which Bruce had to bring to life.'

That was the cover of Queen II (1974), which featured a stark black-

and-white group image of each band member, heads-only save for Freddie, who appears in the centre with his hands folded like wings across his chest. Mick Rock, the photographer, had come up with the idea for that shot.

'The band's brief for that record jacket was short,' Rock adds. 'It would be a gatefold with a black-and-white motif,' says the artist. The band would be featured. It was my problem beyond that. I'd art direct it and photograph it. I had lately made friends with John Kobal, who was an avid collector of early Hollywood stills.'

Kobal, a late Austrian-born Canadian cinema historian and author, was a leading authority on the Golden Age of Hollywood.

'In exchange for a photo shoot with himself, John handed me several prints from his collection,' Rock reveals.

'Among them was a photograph of Marlene Dietrich from the film Shanghai Express, which I had never seen before. Her arms were folded, and she was dressed in black against a black background that was well lighted. Her hands and tilted head appeared to float. I immediately recognized the link. It was one of those instinctive, visceral experiences. Very powerful. Quite clear. Glamorous, mysterious, and timeless. I'd turn it into a four-headed monster. They had no choice but to go for it. As a result, I went to Freddie. He noticed it as well. He realised. He fell in love with it right away. And he sold it to the rest of the band. "I shall be Marlene," he chuckled. "What a delectable thought!"'

Any reservations the members of the band had about pretension were quickly dispelled by Freddie.

'He loved to cite Oscar Wilde,' Rock laughs: "Often, what is considered pretentious today is considered state of the art tomorrow." The crucial thing is to be thought about.'"

This cover served as the basis for Gowers' 'Bohemian Rhapsody' video, which the band realised was a necessary performance as well as promotional tool because performing the song in its whole would be unfeasible. Gowers took a previously constructed image, embellished and developed it, and brought it as far forward as he dared.

'It was the first album that was thrust to the forefront by virtue of a visual,' Vance explained. 'Today, Queen is often regarded as the first band to create a surrealist promotional film, although this was not the case. They were, I believe, predated by Devo', a 1973 American post-punk art rock band who were early pioneers of the music video.

'However, Queen were unquestionably the first band to make a "concept" video. The video brilliantly caught the musical imagery. And, to be honest, it had nothing to do with Freddie. The song was simply the song. The visual interpretation shaped the song into what it is now. Because the images replayed in the listener's head every time the song had an echo. They rapidly become inseparable. You can't hear the song without seeing the images in your head. "Bohemian Rhapsody" could be considered the first single to be "seen" everywhere. Because this was the first video to ever promote music in this manner.'

Mike Appleton remembers the excitement in the OGWT studio when the video arrived.

'A truly fantastic concept,' he remarked. 'I was completely enthralled. All I had to do was display it on the screen. I recall being astounded by Freddie, as if there had never been anything like him before. There hasn't been one since. "Bohemian Rhapsody" helped him develop. He suddenly appeared to be the sole adult in a business ruled by spoiled, whiny children. They understood exactly what they were doing, and they did it with grace. I've never seen a band work as hard as this one.'

Tony Brainsby's initial reaction to the single was 'bizarre'.

'Everyone assumed so. I liked it without knowing why. But that was a watershed moment for me. I had shepherded them from near obscurity to one of the greatest hits of all time. I felt like a father who had just had a child.'

Brainsby's joy was fleeting. Brainsby's position was rendered unsustainable by Queen's new management agreements with John Reid.

'John Reid made it tough for me to continue working with Queen,' he admitted. 'He preferred to deploy his own in-house public relations team. It was declared illegal.'

Brainsby would make his comeback. But, for the time being, if not forever, Queen was in orbit with the man who owned the world's biggest act at the time, the man who made the Rocket Man fly.

A Night at the Opera was released on November 21, 1975, and was celebrated with a magnificent party, as Paul Gambaccini recalls. ..was John Reid's way of saying, "Here you go, Queen are now in Elton's league." Reid knew what he had in Queen, but he didn't realise how fortunate his timing was. If there was ever a time to get Queen on your radar, it was with the release of their fourth album.'

Aside from the professional relationship he would have with the group, Gambaccini built personal friendships that, in Freddie's case, would last a lifetime.

'They were always the poster children for rock musicians who understood what this insane game was all about. They were aware that it was a business. They had no idea they'd become best buddies. All they had to do was get along and appreciate one another. This even-handed, casual attitude got them over obstacles that might have broken up other acts.

'Freddie was the one I was closest to. When you met him, he was one of those individuals who always got right to the heart of the subject. He was very personable and open. I'm not the type to engage in small talk. Part of this, I feel, is because I, like him, am a gay person in the rock world.'

Perhaps Freddie envied Gambaccini's bravery in openly declaring his homosexuality because he yearned to do the same?

'Perhaps. He once told me, "One day, we'll do an interview, and we'll tell it all." We never did. 'But I will admit that he made me feel like a visitor,' Paul recalls, referring to Freddie's promiscuity, which considerably outweighed his own.

'He seemed to be the true homosexual. But, while I was out there being open about it, he was keeping it quiet while being gay with a capital "G". In comparison to him, I was just a little pretender.'

'Bohemian Rhapsody' became Queen's first Number One single five days after the album's release. On a brief twenty-four-date pre-Christmas tour, the band celebrated in style, with an electric Christmas Eve show at Hammersmith Odeon, which was carried by both OGWT and Radio 1.

Three days later, the album became platinum with sales of more than 250,000, which would more than double within weeks. It would also go 56 weeks on the American charts. The New Year brought many more awards, including another 'Ivor' for 'Bohemian Rhapsody'. Unusually for Reid, he purchased ad space in Sounds magazine to congratulate his 'guys' on their accomplishment.

It was time to arrange their second American tour as major rock stars. It would be their most difficult tour to date, visiting nearly every state under the direction of new tour manager Gerry Stickells. Stickells had been both a roadie and tour manager for The Jimi Hendrix Experience, and was purportedly with the star the night he died - however the tragedy was shrouded in mystery, and not something he spoke about often. Stickells stayed with Queen until the band's final tour.

The band perfected the art of the post-gig party on this massively successful US tour. Queen's after-shows became legendary as the greatest in the business. Local dignitaries, celebrities, and party goers would be invited to experience Bacchanalian delicacies wherever the band performed. Journalist Rick Sky recalls a 'small, convert bash' to commemorate the triumph of a show at New York's hallowed Madison Square Garden in his personal homage to Freddie, The Show Must Go On, which was released shortly after the singer's death.

'I'd been invited to New York for an exclusive interview with Freddie and ended up backstage,' Sky explained.

'There were a dozen topless servers with magnums of champagne constantly filling your glass. Nobody was allowed to run out of water. Freddie wore a white vest and held a plastic cup of champagne and a cigarette. He appeared unconcerned and unhurried. He advised me that the key to happiness was to live life to the fullest.

"Excess is part of my nature," he explained. "Dullness is a disease to me." I require peril and excitement. I was not designed to stay inside and watch television. I am undeniably a sexual being. I used to say I would go with anyone, but I've grown more picky. I enjoy being around weird and interesting people because they make me feel more alive. Straight folks boring me to tears. I adore oddballs. I'm a restless and high-strung person by nature, thus I wouldn't make a decent family man. Deep down, I am an extremely emotional person, prone to extremes that are often harmful to both myself and others.

"I live life to the fullest," he stated later, provocatively. "My sexual desire is enormous." I've slept with men, women, and animals, to mention a few. I'll sleep with anything! My bed is so large that I can sleep six people comfortably. I prefer my sex to be uninvolved."'

Freddie's celebrity and money had given him the opportunity to indulge as much as he pleased.

'He was going for it,' Sky claimed. 'However, it must have jeopardised the desire to settle down into a full one-on-one relationship, which we all crave. "When I have a relationship, it is never half-hearted," he remarked. I don't believe in compromise or half-measures. I offer everything I have because that's who I am."'

America, particularly New York, had turned Queen's, particularly Freddie's, heads. He had fallen in love with the city in all of its density and intensity, not to mention its underground gay scene. At day, he shanked it in opulent uptown stores, hotels, and salons, and at night, he prowled the cobblestone streets of the former downtown meat-packing district, now a gentrified enclave, where the most notorious homosexual clubs and bars were located. Although most of these would close in the mid-1980s as a result of the AIDS crisis, they were a magnet for homosexuals and lesbians from all over the country at the time. The Stonewall Riots of June 1969, which began gay liberation, had begun inside New York's most popular illegal gay bar. The dingy Stonewall Inn on Christopher Street off Seventh Avenue in Greenwich Village became famous around the world as the birthplace of homosexual power. The new homosexual glasnost legalised a wealthy gay community industry. Sex palaces, porn theatres, bath houses, leather, S&M, and 'back-room' pubs with names like The Mineshaft and The Anvil proliferated, encouraging the anonymous sexual encounter. Sexually transmitted illnesses were not considered a severe hazard at the time.

According to Mick Rock, who was accompanying him at the time, Freddie first saw one of the Village People at The Anvil club one night. The late 1970s 'YMCA' send-up ensemble, which played with American cultural clichés such as the cowboy, cop, construction worker, biker, Native American, and GI, was a massively popular disco outfit. Freddie was 'utterly mesmerised' by the image of Glenn Hughes, the 'biker,' dancing on the bar, according to Rock.

As Rock put it, 'Freddie was never the same again.'

The Anvil experience was thought to be the inspiration for both Freddie's 'leather' and 'gay clone' appearances. While the 'leather' phase was fleeting, the 'clone' image, which was so far removed from his Seventies Bohemian attitude and favoured closely-cropped hair, a bristly moustache, a strong upper body, and tight denim trousers, would stay. The appearance originally originated in San Francisco, and was dubbed the 'Castro clone' after the Castro district, a once run-down Irish neighbourhood that supplied the Haight-Ashbury hippies. It became Gay Main Street as a result of an influx of homosexual refugees. Initially, the appearance was a mask because straight people did not recognize it as an entirely gay identity. However, from that single image sprang an entire code of homosexual behavior. The colour of the handkerchief hanging from a gay man's back pocket could possibly reveal his sexual orientation.

The 'Hanky Code' or 'Bandana Code' was popular among gays in the late 1970s. Handkerchiefs were worn in the back trouser pocket or looped through belt loops: on the left side of the body for 'tops,' on the right for 'bottoms,' depending on whether you preferred over or underwear. While there is no globally recognized colour code, some of the most well-known ones are yellow for 'watersports,' brown forcat,' black for 'S&M,' purple for 'into piercing,' and red for. ..Let's not go there: light blue for "oral," grey for "bondage," and orange for "anything goes."

To a newly famous Freddie in the late 1970s, one of the most exciting parts of New York was that homosexuality was a political triumph. Gays were out, unified, and in control of their lives and future. Things can only get better from here. So they reasoned. Except for Munich, the frontiers of sexual experimentation may be pushed to extremes not possible in any other city in the globe at the time.

'Compared to how he was in New York or later in Munich, Freddie was fairly well-behaved in London,' Paul Gambaccini remarked.

'Those two places were the epicentres of anonymous, one-time-only sex, which never piqued my curiosity. Freddie obviously loved visiting such locations. It's an entire world, as vast in scope as popular music. I got the idea from him that his experiences in New York were always really crazy, but the gay scene there was much harsher than anywhere else at the time.'

Freddie admitted to'slutting himself' in New York during a conversation with pop journalist turned publisher John Blake.

'It's sin city,' Freddie exclaimed. 'However, you must go at the appropriate moment. It grips you if you stay for too long. It's quite hypnotic. It's all waking up at eight or nine a.m. every day and getting throat shots so I can still sing. It's an actual location. 'I adore it.'

While he loosely admitted to his wild promiscuity here, Freddie kept his cocaine addiction a secret. Aside from the fact that the substance was highly illegal in most countries, including the United Kingdom and the United States, Freddie had never fit the 'druggie' mould and had no desire to do so.

He would have detested being labelled as an addict. He didn't become one; when he decided to stop using the substance, he gave up his habit overnight. But for the time being, he was living the sex, drugs, and rock 'n' roll stereotype. Freddie was addicted to the quick high, the influence that excessive alcohol and cocaine had on his personality and libido. Cocaine increased his self-esteem. It gave him the confidence to play Freddie Mercury.

If Freddie became the ultimate'shopping and fucking' hedonist in New York, it was primarily due to his financial means. Having grown tired of his favourite hotels, the Waldorf Astoria Towers, the Berkshire Place, and the Helmsley Palace, he would purchase a lavish, high-security apartment with stunning views of the Chrysler Building, the Twin Towers, and the Empire State Building. On the forty-third floor of the Sovereign Building at 425 East 58th Street between First Avenue and Sutton Place, and a short walk from Central Park, Bloomingdale's department store and the Carnegie Hall, the apartment boasted a balcony with a view of seven bridges, including the 59th Street bridge made famous by Simon and Garfunkel in the song also known as 'Feelin' Groovy'.

'He was the archetypal cultured person who loved to slum it,' Rick Sky remarked. 'His greatest fantasy is to take a rent boy to the opera. Rudolph Nureyev was akin to Freddie in that he had the uncommon capacity to appreciate both high and low culture.'

Although Freddie admired ballet dancers and rumours of a passionate romance with Nureyev circulated - the Russian had written about his relationship with Freddie and trips to his Kensington house in personal correspondence revealed in 1995 – Freddie's PA Peter Freestone refuted this. Nureyev never came to Garden Lodge, according to Freestone. The ostensible romantic encounter never occurred.

Few knew what drove Freddie's promiscuity and debauchery. The rest of the band merely shrugged and let him carry on. Who were they to judge? The world has progressed in terms of acceptance of sexuality. What Freddie chose to do in his spare time was his business. Sexual orientation was merely one aspect of the overall picture. The supporters tended to embrace what they knew while ignoring the rest. Only the media gets thrilled anytime there is a hint of a scandal. Later, it became clear that Freddie was one of the few rock artists who understood that regular people admired him for his bravery. They admired him for experiencing and tasting life's perils in ways they could never imagine. He was not only delighting his growing audience with superb music and a spectacular spectacle, but he was also giving them the ultimate vicarious thrill.

'We went to a Queen concert, interviewed Freddie, saw the size of all their excesses - and we got to taste the crumbs,' Rick Sky explains.

'That made us, relatively speaking, as privileged as they were. Queens were never self-centred. They were always concerned that everyone else was having as much fun as they were. There was an extraordinary generosity of spirit as well as a sharing of material resources that characterised Queen as the best rock band in the world among all the rock bands we hung around with'.

## 13. CHAMPIONS

In 1976, Queen was at a peak with all four albums in the UK Top Twenty. They toured Japan and Australia, and upon returning to the UK, began working on their fifth album, "A Day at the Races." They released the film "Live at The Rainbow" and Brian May married Chrissy Mullen. John Deacon's "You're My Best Friend" became a Top Ten hit. That summer, Queen played at the Scottish Festival of Popular Music and in Cardiff, followed by a free concert in London's Hyde Park, organised with Richard Branson.

Their Hyde Park gig recalled past concerts by other famous bands and featured a memorable performance by Queen, despite Elton John's absence for his duet with Kiki Dee. Freddie Mercury's engaging stage presence and Queen's ability to experiment with their music, like playing "Tie Your Mother Down" before recording it, were highlights.

Queen's backstage parties became known for their decadence and strip shows, reflecting a different side of the band. Despite rumours about Freddie's sexuality, the band cultivated a reputation for their wild parties. They were unique in staying together after shows, reflecting a strong camaraderie.

The release of "A Day at the Races" was celebrated with a special event, despite the album receiving mixed reactions. "Somebody to Love," the first single, was a hit. The band faced personal and professional changes, with Freddie Mercury ending his relationship with Mary Austin and the rise of punk rock challenging their style.

Queen toured extensively, including in the US, and began recording their next album, facing tax challenges and working in various studios. They maintained a busy schedule, filled with recording, touring, and Freddie Mercury pursuing side projects.

The band's success continued with hits like "We Are the Champions," and they faced controversy over their album "Jazz" and its promotional tactics. Despite backlash and the challenge of constantly topping their previous success, Queen remained a dominant force in the music industry.

# 14. MUNICH

In the late 1970s, Queen's members were experiencing varied personal lives. While Roger, Brian, and John were settling into family roles, Freddie Mercury was fully embracing a more extravagant lifestyle. During their 1979 European tour, the band was working on their "Live Killers" album and later purchased Mountain Studios in Montreux. They also accepted a project to create the soundtrack for the movie "Flash Gordon." In Japan, they were met with adulation, followed by a summer in Munich's Musicland Studios, working with producer Reinhold Mack.

In Munich, the band was influenced by the vibrant local scene, especially Freddie, who was drawn to the city's gay scene. Despite his indulgent lifestyle, Freddie also contemplated a more conventional life, showing interest in family life during visits to Mack's home. The band's work in Munich, guided by Freddie's vision, led to a new musical direction, focusing on simplicity and rhythm.

Freddie's creativity flourished in the studio, but he struggled with a limited attention span. His collaboration with Mack added a new dimension to Queen's sound. The band's time in Munich was not just about music; it was a period of personal and professional growth and exploration.

Freddie also ventured into ballet, participating in a charity performance with the Royal Ballet, where he received a standing ovation. This experience deepened his interest in ballet and led to a lifelong friendship. Despite rumours about his sexuality, Freddie maintained a playful attitude towards public speculation. His foray into ballet was another example of his willingness to embrace new challenges and experiences.

# 15. PHOEBE

Backstage at the Royal Opera House, Freddie met Peter Freestone, a wardrobe assistant and dresser, who quickly became his personal assistant and remained his devoted companion until the end of Freddie's life. Freddie had come to the Opera House to try on outfits for a ballet gala. Peter recalled that Freddie was extremely polite and impressed by the Opera House, which was a departure from his usual sphere.

Peter joined Queen on tour as a wardrobe assistant, eventually becoming Freddie's personal assistant. They bonded over their shared experience of attending boarding schools in India far from home. Peter learned to navigate the world of rock and became responsible for all of Freddie's personal needs, from packing to arranging travel.

Their relationship was a mix of employer and friend, with clear boundaries. Freddie would occasionally express frustration, but they understood each other. Peter never felt like a servant because Freddie treated him well and never expected him to pay for anything

Freddie's personal life was marked by excess and relationships. He had a passionate relationship with Tony Bastin, a DHL courier, and their on-off affair lasted for two years. Freddie's lovers typically had unsophisticated roots, and he liked the stability of a permanent partner.

Freddie was known for his spending sprees and extravagant purchases. He enjoyed giving presents and lived life to the fullest. His obsession with his house, Garden Lodge, was another way to combat boredom.

Despite the band's massive success, Queen members were growing older and had different priorities. Freddie remained focused on music and perfectionism, less interested in celebrity parties and the limelight. He preferred no-strings sex and reserved emotional commitment for close friends.

The band's success continued with hits like "Crazy Little Thing Called Love" and "Another One Bites the Dust," along with successful albums. They toured extensively and ended their longest tour with sold-out shows at Madison Square Garden. Overall, Freddie Mercury's life was a mix of music, excess, and personal relationships, and he remained dedicated to his art and perfectionism throughout his career.

## 16. SOUTH AMERICA

In 1981, Queen embarked on a groundbreaking tour in South America, a region previously untouched by their live performances. The tour, fueled by rumours and anticipation, marked a significant cultural event, especially in Argentina and Brazil, where the band enjoyed immense popularity. Despite previous artists like Earth, Wind & Fire and Peter Frampton performing in South America, Queen's tour was on a much grander scale, planned in large football stadiums due to soccer's immense popularity in the region.

During the tour preparations, Freddie Mercury was busy finalising the purchase of his New York apartment, which was a relief compared to his usual expensive hotel stays. Meanwhile, logistics for the tour were underway, with massive amounts of equipment being shipped from the United States to Rio de Janeiro and Buenos Aires.

Upon arrival in Buenos Aires, Queen received an overwhelming welcome, far surpassing their experiences in other countries like Japan. This tour had a profound influence on the South American music scene, elevating the standards for live performances and impacting the region's cultural landscape. It also coincided with significant political changes in the region, though it's unclear if the band's presence directly influenced these events.

Freddie Mercury's personal life during this period was turbulent, marked by complex relationships and emotional struggles, which seemed to fuel his creative output. Despite the challenges, Queen's performances were electrifying, with Freddie leading the stage with charisma and energy. The band's success in South America was a testament to their global appeal and the universal language of music.

## 17. BARBARA

In April 1981, Roger Taylor of Queen released his solo album "Fun in Space," marking a period of individual artistic exploration for the band members. Meanwhile, Queen was working on the "Hot Space" album in Montreux. The tranquil Swiss town, home to their Mountain Studios, was a favourite spot for rock musicians due to its privacy and acceptance, and also hosted the annual jazz festival.

During this time, Freddie Mercury was involved in the creation of the iconic song "Under Pressure" with David Bowie. The collaboration occurred spontaneously during a jam session and resulted in a significant hit for both artists. Despite challenges in the recording process, the song was successfully completed and released.

Freddie celebrated his 35th birthday extravagantly in New York, reflecting on his changing attitude towards fame and fortune. He sought a more ordinary life outside Queen, contrasting his earlier desire for recognition.

Freddie's personal life in Munich was complex and tumultuous, involving relationships with Winnie Kirchberger, Jim Hutton, and Barbara Valentin, a renowned actress. His relationship with Barbara was particularly intense, marked by shared understanding and a deep connection.

Queen faced difficulties during their Latin American tour, with various mishaps and challenges. The year also saw the emergence of AIDS, initially affecting the gay community but later understood to affect a broader population.

Back in Munich, Freddie's lifestyle was marked by excess and complexity, navigating multiple relationships and personal challenges. He and Barbara shared a unique bond, providing support and understanding to each other amidst their chaotic lives. Overall, this period for Freddie and Queen was one of artistic exploration, personal challenges, and significant changes in their professional and personal lives.


# 18. JIM

John Travolta's portrayal of Tony Manero in "Saturday Night Fever" (1977) sparked a disco fever, with New York City's Studio 54, Le Jardin, and Regine's becoming hotspots for celebrities and the elite. The film, based on Nik Cohn's article, highlighted the escape disco offered from reality, particularly for the gay community.

London's gay scene was less developed, but Jeremy Norman, inspired by New York's disco wave, opened the Embassy Club in London. This club became a hub for diverse and extravagant crowds, including celebrities like Pete Townshend and David Bowie. Stephen Hayter, known as 'Queen of the Night', played a significant role in the club's popularity but tragically became an early victim of AIDS.

Norman later opened Heaven, a large gay club under Charing Cross station, which became a landmark in gay clubbing. Freddie Mercury was a frequent visitor, enjoying the freedom and expression the club offered.

Paul Gambaccini recalls a conversation with Freddie at Heaven in 1984, where Freddie's reckless attitude towards his health and the emerging AIDS crisis became apparent. Freddie, possibly already infected, seemed to accept his fate and continued his extravagant lifestyle.

Freddie's personal life was complex. He had relationships with Barbara Valentin and Winnie Kirchberger, but it was Jim Hutton, whom he met at a gay bar, who became a significant partner. Despite initial hesitations and Freddie's lifestyle, their relationship deepened over time.

By 1987, Freddie was diagnosed with AIDS but kept it private, even from his bandmates. He eventually revealed his illness indirectly during a dinner with the band. Freddie and Jim's relationship became more profound as Freddie's health declined. Jim stayed with Freddie until his death, despite the challenges.

Freddie's household at Garden Lodge consisted of close friends and staff who played various roles in his life. Mary Austin, Freddie's former partner, remained a significant figure, holding a special place in his life and managing his personal affairs.

In summary, the rise of disco culture, particularly in New York and London, created spaces for freedom and expression, especially for the gay community. Freddie Mercury's life during this era was marked by personal and public challenges, profound relationships, and the shadow of the AIDS epidemic.


# 19. BREAK FREE

In 1983, amidst rumours of a split, Queen took a break from touring to focus on solo projects, with each member exploring individual musical interests. Despite thoughts of leaving, they recognized the unique value of their collaboration. That year, Queen faced challenges with their "Hot Space" album and their diminishing popularity in America, although they continued touring and making TV appearances.

Freddie Mercury's personal life was eventful, including a visit to

Michael Jackson's mansion and thoughts of collaborating on music. He also developed a deep interest in opera, particularly inspired by Montserrat Caballé.

Queen's relationship with their American record label Elektra deteriorated, leading them to sign with EMI's American affiliate, Capitol. During this period, they began working on "The Works" album at the Record Plant in Los Angeles. The recording process was like working on solo projects, with each band member bringing their own songs.

The band's reputation in the States suffered further due to their controversial music video for "I Want to Break Free," which featured the members in drag. American audiences did not receive it well, and it impacted their popularity.

In 1984, Queen focused on "The Works" album and its promotion. Their singles like "Radio Ga Ga" and "It's a Hard Life" reflected personal and emotional themes from Freddie's life. Despite setbacks in the U.S., they continued to tour and record, including a controversial performance in Sun City, South Africa, during the apartheid era.

Towards the end of 1984, Queen participated in charity events and released their first Christmas single, "Thank God It's Christmas." Although not a major hit, it became a recurring holiday song. Concurrently, Band Aid's "Do They Know It's Christmas?" dominated the charts, leading to significant historical developments in the music industry.

## 20. LIVE

In 1985, Queen participated in Rock in Rio, the largest rock festival at that time, featuring a lineup of famous artists. Despite Freddie Mercury's immense popularity in South America, his fame meant he was virtually imprisoned by his own celebrity, unable to move around freely due to the intense fan following.

At the festival, Queen experienced a few misinterpretations and technical issues, but overall, their performances were successful. Freddie's style and charisma were particularly noted, with his appearance likened to a Latin Clark Gable. Despite some media exaggerations and misunderstandings during their performances, Queen and Freddie were adored by fans.

Freddie's life offstage was extravagant and indulgent. He threw lavish parties and engaged in a hedonistic lifestyle, often involving casual sexual encounters and substance use. This relentless pursuit of pleasure seemed to indicate an underlying exhaustion and a possible inner conflict.

Meanwhile, Queen faced criticism for their involvement in various projects and their perceived exploitation of Live Aid's success for personal gain. Despite this, the band continued to work on new music, including contributions to the film "Highlander" and other solo projects.

Freddie's 39th birthday was celebrated with an excessive party, which was typical of his extravagant lifestyle. However, his solo career wasn't as successful as he had hoped, with singles from his album "Mr Bad Guy" not performing well in charts.

Queen's participation in the Live Aid concert in 1985 was a notable highlight, with their performance widely praised and considered one of the best live rock performances ever. This success reinvigorated the band, leading to a massive European tour in 1986, which became one of the most ambitious and successful tours of their career. This period was marked by the band's realisation of the importance of staying together and capitalising on their renewed popularity following Live Aid.

## 21. BUDAPEST

"Queen's fourteenth album and the Highlander soundtrack, "A Kind of Magic," was released in May 1986, coinciding with their European tour. The tour, comprising 26 concerts across 11 countries, was a massive success, attracting a million fans. Official photographer Denis O'Regan captured the tour, noting the contrast between the band's wild partying and Freddie Mercury's more subdued nature. Freddie, known for his dynamic stage presence, revealed a quieter side offstage, though he could be temperamental.

The tour was less about the band's earlier excesses and more about a relaxed pace, with Freddie preferring quieter evenings, often playing Scrabble or Trivial Pursuit. The tour's highlight was a lavish party at London's Roof Gardens club, famous for its outrageous atmosphere and celebrity appearances.

The Budapest concert in July 1986 was particularly significant as it was the first major open-air stadium concert by a Western rock group in the Eastern Bloc, drawing 80,000 fans. The event was a cultural milestone, demonstrating Queen's global influence and Freddie's star power. Despite the tour's success, Freddie faced personal challenges, and the concert at Knebworth Park would unknowingly be his last with Queen. The tour ended with a sense of poignancy, as Freddie's health issues began to surface, marking a turning point in his and the band's journey."

## 22. GARDEN LODGE

The Queen machine was continuously active, with Freddie Mercury enjoying a guaranteed income for life. Despite his wealth, Freddie preferred a private life with a small circle of trusted friends and staff, including Mary Austin who managed his household and accounts. Jim Hutton, his partner, was also a significant part of his life, though to Freddie's parents, Jim was presented merely as the gardener due to their religious beliefs.

Freddie's family, including his parents and sister Kashmira, played an important role in his life. He maintained a close but discreet relationship with them, respecting their simple lifestyle and the modest home they chose to keep. His family gatherings were intimate, with his sister Kashmira and her family occasionally visiting.

By 1986, Freddie had grown tired of his earlier, wilder lifestyle and preferred quieter home gatherings. His 40th birthday party was a relatively modest affair, reflective of his changing attitudes and desire for a more settled life. Freddie meticulously cared for his home and valued the close-knit environment at Garden Lodge, where he lived with his staff and friends in a family-like atmosphere.

Despite the joyous occasions, Freddie's life was not without turmoil. In 1986, a sensational news article exposed many personal details of his life, including past relationships and wild nights with celebrities. This betrayal by his former personal manager, Paul Prenter, deeply hurt Freddie and made him wary of trusting new people.

The late 1980s were a challenging time for people with AIDS, with misinformation and discrimination prevalent. Freddie had to navigate these difficulties while maintaining a low profile, partly to protect his family from any potential embarrassment in their community and to fulfil his recording contract obligations.

Queen released the "Live Magic" album in 1986 and decided to take a break for a year. Freddie balanced his work and personal life, spending time with friends, attending to business, and indulging in his hobbies. He lived his life to the fullest despite knowing that his time was limited.


# 23. BARCELONA

Determined to prove himself after his first solo album underwhelmed, Freddie Mercury chose Townhouse Studios in West London for his follow-up project. There, he recorded "The Great Pretender," a hit originally by The Platters. Freddie was so pleased with his version that he filmed an elaborate music video, which included nods to Queen's history and became one of his most beloved promos.

Freddie's admiration for opera singer Montserrat Caballé led to a collaboration on an Olympic anthem. Their meeting in Barcelona was a success, marked by mutual awe and excitement about working together. This partnership culminated in the "Barcelona" album, a unique fusion of rock and opera. Despite logistical challenges, the album was a significant achievement in Freddie's career.

Freddie's personal life was affected by his AIDS diagnosis, prompting a getaway to Ibiza. He remained active, converting cottages in Kensington and planning a conservatory. Despite his illness, he continued to work with Queen, recording "The Miracle" album in a harmonious studio atmosphere. The album was a success, and Freddie found peace and refreshment in Montreux, away from speculation about his health.

Queen was voted 'Best Band of the Decade' and Freddie remained creatively engaged, focusing on promoting Queen's new music and videos. As the 1990s began, Queen started recording "Innuendo," anticipated to be Freddie's final album due to his health. This period marked a blend of creative triumphs and personal challenges for Freddie.


# 24. FOR THE ROAD

Jim Beach negotiated an end to their contract with Capitol. Unknown to the band, Hollywood Records, led by an entertainment lawyer who admired Queen, was interested in signing them. Despite initial doubts, the deal proved hugely successful, especially after the boost from "Bohemian Rhapsody" in the movie "Wayne's World."

Queen's entire catalogue was to be digitally remastered and re-released on CD. Despite Hollywood Records President Peter Paterno's confidence, Disney CEO Michael Eisner was concerned about the deal due to Freddie Mercury's AIDS diagnosis. However, Paterno believed the deal would be profitable regardless of Freddie's health.

As Freddie's health deteriorated, Queen celebrated their 20th anniversary in 1990 with a party at London's Groucho Club, amidst widespread rumours of Freddie's illness, which the band and their team continuously denied. Freddie's aura and charisma were still palpable, even as he faced his mortality.

Throughout his last year, Freddie and the band continued to work on music, including the album "Made in Heaven," released posthumously. Freddie returned to his passion for drawing and painting, creating abstract pieces and spending his final days at Garden Lodge. He cut off contact with many, including his parents, to avoid distressing them with his deteriorating condition. Close friends and caregivers supported Freddie in his last days.

On 23 November, Freddie and his team prepared a public statement acknowledging his AIDS diagnosis, released just before his death. Freddie Mercury passed away on 24 November 1991, leaving behind a profound musical legacy and a lasting impact on his fans and the music world.


# 25. LEGEND

Death, according to Zoroastrians, is not the end of the world, but rather the beginning. Earthly life is regarded to be just a warm-up for the afterlife, where numerous gifts await. Because fire, soil, and water are sacrosanct to Parsees, they are not burnt, interred, or buried at sea.

The body is not maintained because it is viewed as an empty vessel, but is committed for 'celestial burial' and deposited within 'Towers of Silence' beyond city limits. It may also be devoured by birds of prey there, at the mercy of the elements. This technique could not take place in England, not even for a superstar.

'It had to be cremation, and it had to happen as quickly as possible after death,' Peter agreed, signing Freddie's death certificate himself and listing the cause of death as 'a. Bronchopneumonia. b. AIDS,' according to Dr. Atkinson.

A post-mortem examination was not necessary because doctors were there around the clock. As a result, Peter Freestone rushed to make funeral preparations, speaking with Freddie's parents.

'They have to be taken into account. They were burying their son while we were burying a rock star. Naturally, they desired that everything be done in accordance with Parsee tradition. All of their requests were considered.'

'When Freddie died, he told me he wanted to be taken directly out,' Jim added.

'He wanted it to be over as fast and quietly as possible. He would have preferred to be cremated the same day if we had been able to arrange it. Get it over with so that everyone can get back to normal. ..Freddie never wanted people pulling their hair out or gnashing their teeth. Get on with your life. That's what it's there for.'


At 10:00 a.m., Freddie was cremated at West London Crematorium in Kensal Green. on Wednesday, November 27.

'It was absolutely flawless, just like Freddie would have wanted it,' Peter says with a smile. 'For the flowers alone, there were five Daimler hearses. Freddie was in a Rolls-Royce hearse, followed by four automobiles. His plain, pale oak coffin with a solitary red rose on top was carried in by pallbearers to Aretha Franklin's "You've Got a Friend." We were all following. There were fourteen people on the "friends" side and roughly thirty people on the "family" side.'

In his green Bentley, Elton John arrived. Brian arrived with his on-again, off-again lover Anita Dobson (now his wife). Mary Austin, who was expecting her second child, Jamie, arrived with Dave Clark. Jim Callaghan, Queen's loyal security guard, stood calmly at the chapel's door, waiting to greet and accompany Freddie's parents in.

'When the coffin vanished, we played a recording of Verdi's aria from Il Trovatore, 'D'Amor sull'ali rosee,' sung, of course, by Montserrat Caballé. That was Freddie's favourite musical piece of all time. He'd frequently go into the studio, switch it on, and crank it up so loud that you could hear the musicians flipping the pages of their music and even moving their seats. 'It was quite emotional, and I was quite sad,' Peter said. I needed to be alone. My mother was laid to rest at that crematorium. I recall running down to where her ashes were interred and asking her to watch after him.'

Outside the crematorium, Freddie's flower tributes took up more than a quarter of an acre. White dahlias and lilies with the message, 'To our very loving son Freddie,' came from his parents. Mum and Dad, we will always love you'. Yellow roses from David Bowie. A heart of pink rosebuds with the words 'Thank you for being my friend' from Elton John. I will always love you'. Boy George's tribute simply stated, "Dear Freddie, I love you." Mary Austin's wreath was a yellow and white rose cushion with the note 'For my dearest, with my deepest love, from your Old Faithful'. Her son's wreath read, 'To Uncle Freddie with love from your Ricky'. 'Goodbye old friend, peace at last!' read Roger Taylor's heartfelt farewell.All of the flowers were ultimately donated to hospitals in London.

Back at the house, Jim went into the garden alone since he couldn't bear the gathering inside.

'I had lost my father years before,' he explained, 'but I wasn't in Ireland at the time. As a result, Freddie was the closest person to me who died. It struck me hard.'

Jim would become enraged by the words and actions of others in the coming weeks. According to the press, Dave Clark stated that he was the only person in the bedroom when Freddie died.

'He wasn't the only one in the room,' Jim pointed out. 'However, it was quoted everywhere.'

The error must have irritated the sensitive and kind Clark, for Jim received a lovely card from him on his birthday.

'The inscription he scribbled inside said "You were there," and I don't see why anybody would think otherwise. When Freddie was sick, Dave was fantastic. He'd come around to the house all the time and help out. Yes, he sat by Freddie's bed for hours to give us a respite. Dave was present the night Freddie died. But not in the way he described.

'Freddie's favourite cat Delilah hadn't been on his bed all day, which was unusual. She slept in that room. It was practically where she lived. She was on the floor at the foot of his bed that evening. I went to get her. At the time, Dave was holding one of Freddie's hands. With it, he stroked Delilah. As Dave did so, Freddie gave a slight nod of acknowledgment. Then Freddie expressed a desire to use the restroom. I dashed downstairs to summon Peter to assist me; Freddie had wet the bed and we needed to change the sheets. Dave exited the room to maintain his dignity. Freddie passed away at that point.'

Jim would never fully recover from his grief.

'There are still times when I'm pottering around in the garden and Freddie's face when he died will come to mind,' he told me in Ireland. 'I can consciously forget what happened, but not psychologically. It is difficult to forget. I learnt so much from him, not the least of which was to keep a cheerful attitude. "But you can, don't you see?" was Freddie's constant response. You've got this. Put your mind to it, and you'll see what you're capable of." That was one of his most endearing qualities.'

Jim died in Ireland in 2010 from lung cancer.

Barbara Valentin was left to deal with her sadness alone in Munich. She'd purchased 'the black attire,' as well as booked and paid for her plane ticket. She was preparing to leave for the airport when she received a phone call ordering her to stay away. She refused to tell who had made the call, and Peter Freestone said he couldn't remember. It was almost certainly one of Jim Beach's squad. Mary Austin was to be 'the widow' that day, and Barbara was not invited.

'I couldn't even come to bury him,' she sobbed. 'After everything we'd been through. The agony was excruciating. I've never gotten over it. I'd never felt love like I did with Freddie, and I haven't felt it since. I haven't gone looking for it. Enough was enough. He was my life's greatest love. He is still there. To have what I had, twenty women would have to live a hundred years. It is preferable to cease at the appropriate time. That's probably what he did as well.'

'At least Freddie got to do what he always felt a star should do,' she continued. He used to remind me that you can't afford to tumble from

152

the top or become less outstanding than you were. Fame had made him the most lonely person on the planet. To compensate for this, his life grew increasingly out of control. Freddie was overcompensating for his loneliness by going to extremes. The cost he paid was the most heinous. I'm sure he wouldn't have intended it that way. He did, however, get his way. He desired immortality, and that is exactly what he received.'

Barbara died after a stroke in 2002 in Munich.

Garden Lodge never returned to "normal." Mary gave the idea that she wanted the others to leave as she prepared to move in. Jim assumed he would be permitted to stay as long as he pleased. In the end, he was ordered to leave right away.

'And me. 'And Joe,' Peter Freestone reflected regretfully. 'We didn't have someplace else to go and needed some time to figure things out. We would have departed sooner or later. ..Mary's actions were obviously perplexing.'

'How on earth could the three of us be treated the way we were, after all we had been through with Freddie?' Jim stated. 'It made no sense. 'I left that place with nothing, not even my personal belongings.'

The ensuing legal and financial battles left Freddie's former caregivers in limbo, and Barbara Valentin nearly homeless. She defeated the opposition with the assistance of her Garden Lodge pals. Freddie's will left many unanswered questions, some of which would never be answered.

Jim Hutton later explained that his motivation for writing his memoir was anger, not money. He couldn't see any other way to let the world know the truth.

'I suspect Jim Beach was upset that my book damaged "the myth of Freddie,"' Jim speculated. 'All it did was restore him to his original human state. It was telling the truth. Beach wanted audiences to believe that sweet Mary Austin was Freddie's love, and what a wonderful, tragic, romantic story it was. I believe that whether or not Freddie was gay is irrelevant to the fans. I also feel that fans want to hear the whole truth, good and bad.'

Peter Freestone had the same opinion. Freddie would have been horrified to see the people he cared about fall out after his death.

'Those involved must live with themselves. Jim [Hutton] had "a very vivid imagination," Mary once said. I have known Jim for a long time and never knew him to be anything but completely honest. Jim, like mine, had a pure conscience.'

Was his ashes scattered on Freddie's 'Swan Lake' in Montreux? Is he kept alive in an urn on his parents' mantelpiece? Had they been sent to a beach in Zanzibar to be offered to the sea, conveyed to his Aunt Sheroo in India for safekeeping, or buried behind a cherry tree in the grounds of Garden Lodge, as Jim Hutton claimed? Could they be hidden beneath the grave of an unknown deceased in Surrey's Brookwood Civil and Military Cemetery, which has a designated Parsee plot? Gita Choksi, Freddie's old school friend from St Peter's, Panchgani, believes so. Gita bumped into a caretaker on the grounds on her first-ever visit to her own father's grave at that cemetery, and the two struck up a conversation. 'Freddie Mercury's ashes are interred over there,' he explained.

'I was utterly stunned and overcome,' Gita admitted.

'The caretaker plainly had no means of knowing anything about my relationship with Freddie and had no need to lie. I hadn't seen my old school friend in years, and now he was buried just a few feet from my own father's. I am completely certain that it is true. I doubt the caretaker, a Parsee like Freddie, would tell me such a thing if it weren't true. It was the most incredible thing that had ever happened to me. 'However, I was glad for it.'

Could the man have made a mistake? It is conceivable. Surprisingly, when I visited the Brookwood Parsee plot, a caretaker told me the same thing. It occurred to me that this could be a purposeful tactic to confuse fans. Certainly not. ..While Peter Freestone was not startled to hear Gita's story, he was unable to validate it. 'I honestly don't know. I believe his ashes were divided, with the parents receiving some and Mary receiving some. ..But who am I to say? Only they know for certain.'

Soon after Freddie's death, 'Bohemian Rhapsody' was re-released as a Christmas 1991 single. It quickly rose to the top of the charts, raising almost a million pounds for the Terrence Higgins Trust AIDS charity. The Magic Johnson Foundation distributed revenues from the re-release of Queen's iconic single to AIDS charities across the United States.

On April 20, 1992, the band was ready to send Freddie go with a rock 'n' roll send-off, with a show that would later be voted the best live rock event of the 1990s. Brian, who regarded Freddie's death as "like losing a brother," insisted that the Freddie Mercury Tribute Concert at Wembley Stadium on Easter Monday that year was "not Queen," despite the fact that the majority of those who performed Queen songs. Even though no lineup had been announced, 72,000 tickets were sold out in two hours on the day the performance was announced. The event would be carried on radio and television in 76 countries, and David Mallet would record it for a documentary.

The spectacular presentation began with recorded footage of Freddie performing vocal scales. 'Under Pressure' by Annie Lennox and David Bowie, 'I Want It All' by Roger Daltrey. Extreme performed 'Hammer to Fall,' George Michael and Lisa Stansfield collaborated on 'These Are the Days of Our Lives,' and Elton John and Axl Rose performed 'Bohemian Rhapsody,' respectively. 'Who Wants to Live Forever' was chosen by Seal. Mott the Hoople's Mick Ronson and Ian Hunter deviated from the standard format to pay respect to David Bowie's 'All the Young Dudes'. So did Robert Plant, who sang 'Thank You' by Led Zeppelin as well as 'Innuendo' and 'Crazy Little Thing Called Love'. But it was Liza Minnelli's magnificent rendition of 'We Are the Champions' that blasted them all off the stage.

What about Dave Clark, Peter Straker, Tony Hadley, and Elaine Paige? Are you familiar with Aretha Franklin, Prince, and Michael Jackson? Many of us were taken aback by the unexplained absence of singers who had meant so much to Freddie, as well as the fact that the metal' part of the lineup was possibly not what Freddie would have preferred. Brian and Roger preferred the music of Guns N' Roses, Metallica, and Def Leppard. Many of the acts who did play were said to have been picked because their own sound was influenced by Queen. Others think that the Tribute event was really about Brian, Roger, and John inviting their beloved lead man back into the Queen fold, where he belonged in their hearts, and about a look back at the band's original flavours, ethos, and aspirations.

Tim Rice claims that Elaine Paige was 'wounded' when Liza Minnelli was selected to perform at the tribute instead of her. Many people were surprised by the lack of an 'out' gay element to celebrate Freddie's lifestyle - Boy George, Holly Johnson, Jimmy Somerville, Leee Johns. Pavarotti, Carreras, and Domingo delivering the classical arias Freddie admired would have looked and sounded completely out of place against the lineup that did appear. Montserrat Caballé has stated that she had full commitments to EXPO in Seville, singing live every night during its inaugural week, which began on the same date as the tribute event. She had expressed a desire to participate in Freddie's concert via satellite. However, because the concert was being broadcast live throughout the world, a satellite link into London could not be established. Even the late Hollywood actress and AIDS activist Dame Elizabeth Taylor couldn't make up for La Stupenda's absence in her heartbreaking address to the audience.

George Michael, who stole the stage with 'Somebody to Love,' mirroring the band's Live Aid victory seven years earlier, stated that he was "living out a childhood fantasy."

'When I think of Freddie, I think of everything he taught me about craft,' George explained. 'It was an incredible feeling just to sing those songs, especially "Somebody to Love." It was most likely my proudest moment in my career.'

'George Michael at the tribute concert was incredible,' said Peter Paterno. 'It did cross my mind, and I'm sure many others', that they should really consider having him take Freddie's place. In the end, I suppose no one ever could.'

Spike Edney, who played keyboards with Mike Moran, was

disappointed by the post-concert backlash, in which many critics criticised contributors for falling short of Freddie's expectations. Those who were disappointed failed to recall or comprehend that just a few performers in rock history have possessed Freddie's amazing vocal range.

'It might not be fair to say that none of those great singers could sing any of the songs as well as Freddie,' he argues. 'However, I know that many of them felt as if they were under his shadow. Of course, he would have appreciated it. It would have made him happy to see them all suffer. He would have enjoyed the agony of not being able to match his keys as well as enjoying it for what it was - a wonderful homage!'

The scene at the after-show party at Brown's nightclub summed up the event, according to Spike.

'I saw Roger lean up against the wall, staring into space,' I said. Then I noticed Brian doing the same thing a few feet away. I approached them. "How are you feeling?" I said. "Can't feel anything," said one of them. Nobody has any recollection of it. You couldn't possibly take it all in. After that, it was, "God, what have we done for the past month?" So, what are we going to do now?"'

The gears of fundraising were in motion. The Mercury Phoenix Trust, founded in 1992 to handle funds from the concert and other sources, used the phoenix from Queen's crest, which Freddie designed at the start of the band's existence, as its insignia. To this day, the trust raises funds for AIDS-related projects all across the world.

The Mercury Phoenix Trust received profits from the Five Live mini album contributed by George Michael, Lisa Stansfield, and Queen. The Trust received a significant boost in April 2002 when the performance was published on DVD to commemorate the charity's tenth anniversary. It debuted at the top of the UK chart. Money is still flowing into the fund after twenty years.

Without a doubt, Jim, the devastated lover, began his selected 1994 memoir with the purpose of crafting a heartfelt tribute to an adored companion. A co-writer muddied this by focusing on more sensational aspects of the connection as well as intimate details of Freddie's final days.

As a result, Jim was expelled from the Queen's camp. This reaction, which left him befuddled and confused, was most likely caused by Freddie's bandmates, management, family, and friends' grief. It was difficult for them to witness the graphic facts of Freddie's death exposed for all to see.

I had no doubt that the love Jim claimed to have felt for Freddie was genuine during the time I spent with him in lovely County Carlow, in the southeast of Ireland, where he lived out his days in a comfortable home built with Freddie's £500,000 legacy. He was a pleasant and nice man who was pleased with his station in life. He was forever thankful to Freddie for exposing him to the celebrity lifestyle, he told me. He proudly displayed his lavender 'Blue Moon' roses in his garden, which Freddie enjoyed.

Given Jim's Catholic upbringing and the fact that his mother was still alive when he published, writing the book must have required enormous fortitude.

'I did speak about it with my family,' he admitted. 'In a sense, I begged for their consent. I shouldn't have been concerned. They simply stated that they were available to me and that was the end of it.'

Jim was aware that Freddie was in a more difficult situation due to his family's religious beliefs.

'But Freddie didn't practise Zoroastrianism,' Jim reasoned, and Peter Freestone concurred. 'Because Freddie's parents cremated him in accordance with the faith, it was presumed that he practised,' Jim continued.

'But he never worshipped in all the years I knew him. I'm not familiar with his family's religion. We never talked about it. But I do recall lying in bed next to dad at night and hearing him pray. Which language is it? It is written in English. To whom? I'm not sure. When

I'd question who he was talking to, he'd merely shrug and answer, "I'm saying my prayers."

Following Freddie's death, Queen Productions' offices on Pembridge Road were closed. Mountain Studios closed after David Richards relocated his production facilities to the Alps above Montreux. All that remains is the severely graffitied doorway (and the ghosts of the studio). Many people thought the Queen story would stop with Freddie's death, but they were wrong.

Queen's fifteenth studio album, Made in Heaven, debuted at number one in 1995, four years after Freddie's death. It is an impeccable compilation prepared with labour and passion that is estimated to have sold twenty million copies globally. It is a Requiem to and a showcase for the diva in Freddie, brimming with vitality and mortality. 'Mother Love' is a standout track for me. Freddie's haunting vocal draws us back on a channel-surfing rewind into a blast of incandescent live Queen, an echoed riff from 'It's a Kind of Magic,' and a shred of Gerry Goffin/Carole King's 'Goin' Back,' by Freddie, released as Larry Lurex in Queen's early Trident days. ..'I believe I'm returning to the things I learned so well in my childhood. ..' A heart-tugging infant cry plays the song to a ghostly end, which definitely symbolises his death as the singer's rebirth.

Another favourite on this album is Freddie's farewell song, 'A Winter's Tale,' which he penned and composed in his Montreux apartment overlooking the lake he adored. The lyrics, which describe what he saw through his window, reflect the serenity and contentment he discovered there toward the end. The song's title, whether intended or not as a reference to William Shakespeare's romance 'The Winter's Tale,' indicates maybe more about Freddie's early musical inspiration. Polixenes, King of Bohemia - an old realm roughly equivalent to the modern-day Czech Republic - is one of Shakespeare's characters. As a result, 'Bohemian Rhapsody' may have sprouted. If, as many Bard scholars believe, this play was an allegory about Anne Boleyn's tragedy, the character Perdita was modelled on the daughter of Anne and King Henry VIII, who would become Elizabeth I, England's Queen. ..Is Freddie's farewell offering packed with the band's original biggest hit? It's not unthinkable.

There are other memorials, including Irena Sedlecka's Freddie statue, which stands on the shores of Lake Geneva in Montreux. Montserrat Caballé launched it on November 25, 1996, the fifth anniversary of Freddie's death. The Mayor of Montreux inaugurated the ceremony, which was attended by Freddie's parents, his sister Kashmira, Montreux Jazz Festival founder Claude Nobs, and Brian and Roger. The statue is still one of Switzerland's most popular tourist attractions. It has also become the focal point of Queen fans' annual pilgrimages to celebrate their idol's birthday in September.

'Unveiling the statue was one of my most difficult times,' Brian told Q magazine in 2011. 'Obviously, it's a lovely memorial, and the ceremony was moving, but I was instantly overtaken with rage. I said, "This is all that's left of my friend, and everybody's thinking it's normal and fabulous, but it's actually awful that I'm looking at a piece of bronze which is the image of my friend, and my friend isn't here any more " .

Maurice Bejart of the Bejart Ballet of Lausanne choreographed a special Ballet for Life, 'Le Presbytère n'a rien perdu de son charme ni le jardin de son éclat' ('The Presbytery has lost none of its charm, nor the garden its sparkle'), five years after Freddie's death, to celebrate the lives of Freddie and the Bejart's principal, Jorge Donn. The poignant work, which includes Queen songs and Mozart compositions, begins with 'It's a Beautiful Day,' the first track on Made in Heaven, and ends with 'The Show Must Go On,' the closing track on Innuendo, Queen's final album during Freddie's lifetime. It was initially played in Paris in January 1997, in the presence of Madame Chirac (wife of the then-French President), with Elton John, Brian, Roger, and John Deacon. This was the bassist's final live performance with the band.

Following Freddie's death, John experienced severe depression. Freddie's death brought back recollections of emotions John had not dealt with since the death of his own father when he was eleven. He once went to a lapdancing club and fell in love with a twenty-five-year-old dancer, lavishing her with an apartment, a car, and expensive gifts. After the ill-advised relationship ended, John was understandably eager to retire with his wife and family. He formally departed the band in 1997.

'He's quite private now,' Brian observed. 'When there is a business discussion, he communicates via email, but that's it.'

Brian and Roger were far from ready to let go. The right project would present itself in due course.

Brian sang 'God Save the Queen' on the roof of London's royal house in June 2002 (in tribute to Jimi Hendrix, he said) to kick off Party at the Palace, a concert commemorating Her Majesty Queen Elizabeth II's Golden Jubilee. At the Fender Strat Pack event in 2004, he collaborated for the first time with former Free and Bad Company frontman Paul Rodgers. Brian convinced Paul to play with Queen at their entrance into the UK Music Hall of Fame, citing their apparent chemistry. Brian, Roger, and Paul then announced a global tour as 'Q + PR' in 2005, emphasising that Paul was not replacing Freddie, but that the idea was a variant on a subject. In 2005, they performed at a concert in South Africa for Nelson Mandela's 46664 AIDS awareness campaign, after which they toured together for the remainder of the year, with Spike Edney joyously returning to the keyboards.

Q + PR then embarked on a twenty-three-city North American tour. They appeared in Hyde Park for Nelson Mandela's 90th birthday celebration two years later, bringing their tumultuous South African adventure to a magnificent close. They then embarked on a full-fledged European tour. Although the collaboration has come to an end for the time being, both parties believe that the agreement remains open. Meanwhile, all pursue separate projects, with Brian collaborating with West End and Broadway star Kerry Ellis on a sell-out musical-theatre-meets-rock production titled 'Anthems' in 2011.

On the eighteenth anniversary of Freddie's death, November 24, 2009, 2,000 Queen fans from around the world gathered in Feltham town centre to witness the unveiling of a granite Hollywood Star-style plaque dedicated to her son's memory by Brian and Freddie's mother. It was the first memorial to the Queen frontman in the United Kingdom (excluding the mock-up statue greeting fans to We

Will Rock You atop the Dominion Theatre on Tottenham Court Road).

'Feltham was his first home in England after we arrived from Zanzibar, and it was here that he began to explore his musical future,' recalled Jer Bulsara, 87.

'Freddie, we chased your goal, our dream, and we love you and will always love you,' Brian remarked. 'We are delighted to pay tribute to you in this way.'

'Stormtroopers in Stilettos' (the title is drawn from Queen's third album, Sheer Heart Attack, 1974's tune 'She Makes Me') is a nostalgic international touring exhibition of Queen's early days. It opened in 2011 to mark the band's fortieth anniversary, a year of celebrations that also saw them secure a new record deal with Island Records via Universal.

GK Films announced a blockbuster Hollywood film based on Freddie's life in late 2010. The Freddie Mercury biopic directed by Graham King is co-produced by Robert de Niro's TriBeca Films and Queen Films. Borat and Bruno star Sacha Baron Cohen plays Freddie, with a scenario by Peter Morgan, author of several outstanding screenplays including The Queen, Frost/Nixon, and The Last King of Scotland.

'Freddie Mercury was an awe-inspiring performer,' said King,'so with Sacha starring in the role, coupled with Peter's writing and Queen's support, we have the right combination to portray the true tale behind their success.'

Morgan's story takes the band back to the early 1980s, when they had tarnished their reputation in America and were in decline. Their peak years had passed, and each member was pursuing solo endeavours. Then, when Geldof unveiled Live Aid, Queen accepted his vision and stunned the world at Wembley Stadium. They plan and start on a big international 'comeback' tour, re-awakening to their combined power, and look forward to a robust second innings. However, Freddie succumbs to AIDS, and the dream is ruined. ..The film will be released in the summer of 2012, just in time for the twenty-first anniversary of Freddie's death.

Queen's global popularity and effect have surged since Freddie's death, thanks in no small part to the amazing success of their stage musical We Will Rock You. It was written to iconic Queen songs and set in a futuristic parallel reality where rock music has been prohibited and the Bohemians, a group of music-loving rebels, are looking for a hero. The 'jukebox theatre' production has performed to continually packed houses since its 2002 debut at London's Dominion Theatre, Tottenham Court Road, and shows no signs of slowing down. It has been staged in 27 countries; it received the BBC Radio 2 Olivier Audience Award in March 2011, and will be followed by a long-awaited film adaptation in 2013.

We Will Rock You may not be for everyone. Indeed, Brian and Roger have been accused of 'selling out' by some. What does it matter? Queen does not. The popularity of the show speaks for itself. 'Fuck 'em if they don't get it,' Roger says.

'We Will Rock You's crucial function has been in delivering Queen's amazing music to millions of young people who weren't born while Freddie was alive, and when the original band were still touring,' says Paul Gambaccini.

How would Freddie react if Queen became even more popular today than they were during his lifetime?

'He'd adore it,' says Paul Gambaccini. 'He would adore it. He's bigger than Liza Minnelli: what a kick that would have been for him. He was a sucker for divas. They were adored. Liza and Montserrat were two of his favourite girlfriends. He'd be overjoyed that his oversized projection of himself is so highly regarded. I mean, I receive Facebook friend requests from young European men who know I knew Freddie. This group's idol is Peter Freestone. It's a profession. They put on the dress-ups, tributes, Freddie-for-a-Day (when fans all around the world dress up as their idol on Freddie's birthday to raise money for the Mercury Phoenix Trust), and so on. It's enthralling. When Freddie was active, none of them were alive, or they were unaware. They are reacting to the historically preserved Freddie Mercury, rather than to a man they would have known.'

Those who are still alive go about their lives, which will never be ordinary. Today, John Deacon is a peaceful family guy, his Queen crazy relegated to the top shelf of his tormented psyche. Brian, a Commander of the Order of the British Empire for Services to the Music Industry, enjoys his second wife Anita, his three grown children, astronomy, and the preservation of foxes. Roger married his young girlfriend Sarina after six years together and had five children at the time of his divorce from Debbie. Music is still important to both Roger and Brian.

Queen has surpassed The Beatles to become the official UK album chart leaders. Their Greatest Hits album was the best-selling album in the United Kingdom in 2006, selling over 5,407,587 copies. Their Greatest Hits II album came in seventh place, selling over 3,631,321 copies. The band has sold over eighteen million albums, eighteen million singles, and ten million DVDs worldwide, making them one of the world's best-selling rock acts. Their total album sales are believed to be over 300 million globally, with 32.5 million sold in the United States alone. Queen is also the only band in which every member has written at least one chart-topping single. Both the New York Yankees and Manchester United football club adopted 'We Will Rock You' as their anthem. "We Are the Champions" is still the most-played Queen song of all time, with sports fans all around the world chanting it. Freddie called it "the most egotistical and arrogant song I ever wrote."

'In some ways, I feel like Freddie is still here, because his music is still here,' says his sister Kashmira. 'He was my brother, but he was also a megastar. Simply said, I have no idea what it was like to have a regular brother. That's because my own brother was exceptional.'


'Freddie was my best friend,' Roger Taylor admitted candidly. 'I've never recovered from his death. Neither of us has. I believe we all expected to get over it soon, but we misjudged the impact his death had on our lives. It's still tough for me to talk about. Our present and future are incomprehensible without Freddie. I deal with that on a daily basis.'

He misses Freddie because he is the soul behind the superstar: a very human man who fell for a fantasy. Millions were delighted, much to the chagrin of some. It was entirely on his terms. He expected no sympathy despite his lack of apology. If he felt confined by the contradictions that shaped him at times, his songs set him free.

To the crying clown who got the last laugh. ..and, moving forward, to Brian and Roger in his memory. Can anyone criticise them as torchbearers? Not me.

Printed in Great Britain
by Amazon